2012 : A Guide to Spiritual Awareness

'CHANGE HAS BEGUN'

Jay Hill and Michelle Kraus
Foreword by Amy Farrar

INNERCIRCLE PUBLISHING

2012: **A Guide to Spiritual Awareness**
Copyright © 2008 Jay Hill and Michelle Kraus

ISBN: 1-882918-17-7

Edition 1

EDITED BY: Amy Farrar
PAGE DESIGN BY: Chad Lilly
COVER CREATION BY: Chad Lilly
ORIGINAL COVER DRAWING BY: Michelle Kraus

All Rights reserved. No part of this book may be reproduced in any form or by electronic or mechanical means, including information storage and retrieval systems, without permission in writing from the publisher, except by a reviewer who may quote a brief passage in a review. The names of individuals have been changed to preserve confidentiality.

ARE YOU AWARE?
WWW.INNERCIRCLEPUBLISHING.COM

TABLE OF CONTENTS

7 : FOREWORD

11 : INTRODUCTION

19 : CHAPTER 1 - Getting Rid of Stuff - The Beginning

32 : CHAPTER 2 - Fear and Greed

40 : CHAPTER 3 - Forgiving Yourself for Your Mistakes

52 : CHAPTER 4 - Moving On

60 : CHAPTER 5 - Returning to a Spiritual Community

74 : CHAPTER 6 - The Path of Peace

87 : CHAPTER 7 - Dealing with Society

99 : CHAPTER 8 - Raising Your Consciousness in Preparation for 2012

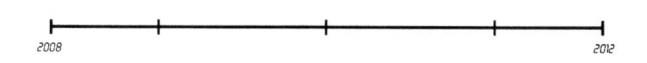

ACKNOWLEDGMENTS

First and foremost, we would like to thank with great humility the messengers who deemed us worthy of receiving their messages and asked for our help to distribute the messages in the book.

Michelle would like to thank her parents Cal and Irene for being supportive in all ways of this project. Michelle would also like to especially thank her husband Mike and daughter Maija for their patience and supportive love during the sometimes trying times of the writing of this book. And as always, a thank you goes to the people who were her second family and friends who listened and accepted her for who she is. Thank You for believing in me.

Jay would like to thank all of the people who helped make this possible. These people include his family and friends who believed in him, and his supervisor Andrea at his work for being so understanding and all the people in his life who regardless if they knew it or not were his teachers. A special big Thank You to his cousin Linda for everything that she did to support this project. Jay would also like to thank Dr. Chris Grams for helping him look at love in a whole different way and showing him how to love with his heart, and for also introducing him to people who helped facilitate the channeling process.

We would both like to thank Drs. Diane and Loren Mickelson for the psychic work they did that helped open and remove blocks in us both so that we could more clearly receive messages. What they did not only helped with the book but helped us in all areas of our lives.

And a special mention and thank you to Amy Farrar. Amy edited the book and through her professionalism and knowledge of the writing business she showed us and taught us much. Amy embraced the project and believed in it and was supportive and patient with our want and needs. She wrote the forward and has started as we have to live as the book asks. Thank you Amy

We would very much like to thank the universe for the abundance we have received in all areas of our life.

FOREWORD

When I was first approached by Jay to work on this book, I wasn't sure what to think. Although I had edited books of a spiritual nature before, I had never edited a strictly channeled book in which much of the information in it was sent by people who had passed on, spiritual guides, and what many of us think of as angels.

But as I began working on the book, I was filled with this overwhelming feeling of trust, not only in Jay and Michelle, but in the book's content and its other authors — the spiritual beings that have brought us this message. In the often unpredictable world of freelance writing and editing, finding clients that we freelancers can trust right away doesn't happen very often. And although I consider myself a fairly New Agey type of person, I also have an analytical mind that usually discounts theories and books about the end of life on Earth as we know it.

This book is not about the end. It is about the beginning—the beginning of a new way of thinking, feeling, and living among the human race on this planet we call our home. Although the authors of the book (and by authors I mean Jay, Michelle, and the spiritual beings who borrowed them to channel this information to you) refer to 2012 as a time of chaos that will result from wars and natural disasters, that time is already upon us, and each of us must take it upon ourselves to do what we can to heal our planet, ourselves, and each other. This is a book about spiritual awakening.

As such, one of the most potent messages in the book is to love they neighbor, a message given by Jesus that most of us in the New Age community take very seriously. Can love conquer all? Yes, I believe that it can. I believe that if we love ourselves, others, and the planet, that we all will come through this into a new world that we can bring into being.

As the authors state in the book, we are already embroiled in tremendous change. Even if you don't believe that spiritual forces are and will be at work over the next decade, you would have to have your head in the sand not to acknowledge the huge changes that are going on right now due to global warming, which was the subject of the first book I wrote (which was part of the reason the universe threw us all together to work on this book).

As the authors suggest, start by unplugging from the unhealthy brainwashing we all receive to be good little consumers; really learn about sustainable living to the best of your ability—how to grow your own food; how to rely on your local community for support and help; and how to survive without electricity or running water in your home. This last point may be alarming, and most Americans reading this may even laugh at it, but it is a very real possibility in a war-torn world ravaged by ongoing natural disasters, even here in the United States. Of course this book states this will happen on a much bigger scale, than say, New Orleans.

How it happens really isn't the point. War and environmental degradation are real world problems that are already at work. 2012 means different things to different people. Many reference it as the end of the Mayan calendar. Although this has been interpreted very negatively by a lot of people, no one knows for sure exactly what the end of the Mayan calendar means. Much of the Mayans' writings were destroyed by invaders and there is no concrete evidence of what the end of their very accurate calendar means. But whether the chaos that already seems to be happening (or at the very least has happened since the dawn of recorded history) means the end of the Mayan calendar, the end times predicted in The Bible, or aliens coming from outer space (for either good or bad reasons), there are a few things we can start doing now, and those are the very valuable lessons outlined in this book.

FOREWORD

One thing is clear—we are at a point in our history where some very big decisions are going to have to be made if we want our planet and our people to survive and thrive. Make the decision suggested in this book and slow down to think about who you are, what you are here for, and who you want to be. Don't let the frantic pace of your life keep you from seeing the reality of it. The decisions we make in the next few years will be important not only for our survival, but for our collective internal evolution.

There's no question that all this change can be very scary. But I truly believe that if we can have the courage to say no to what is happening to our planet and our people the world over, if we can say no to money ruling our lives, and if we can find our spirituality and really incorporate it into our lives, that we can change not only ourselves, but the world.

— Amy Farrar
2008

INTRODUCTION

This book is a guide to simple, slower, and more aware living during this critical time in Earth's history. The information in this book was channeled through us from spiritual sources outside of ourselves, the authors. We refer to the spiritual entities who delivered this information as healers or messengers, but some people refer to others like them as spiritual guides and angels. It is our collective goal to teach you about awareness and how we treat ourselves, others, and the planet.

We asked the messengers if 2012 would be important. They answered with a definitive, "Very much so." This is a profoundly difficult time in the history of the human race. Human beings are being challenged now like they never have been before, by global warming and other environmental problems, and by a spiritual vacuum created by a frenzy of consumerism that is fueling greed, isolation, intolerance, and war. Now is a pivotal time in which we as a race can soften the changes that are coming by relying more on each other as we once did and by learning to become aware of the spiritual guidance that is being sent our way.

INTRODUCTION

Some people have referred to the changes that are coming in a sort of doomsday-like context, but the messengers have assured us that if we take their advice and do what they say, we can weather the changes into an enlightened era. The messengers do not tell you this to alarm you, but to help you make the transition into a much more loving, peaceful existence that will involve living at a higher vibrational frequency that rejects darkness and negativity.

One of the primary messages we received is this:

"You have lost appreciation for the ability to live. You have been placed on Earth for a purpose and we would like you to achieve that purpose. This book is a glimpse of our expectations for proper living. We have light and very little else. Material things are of no value to us. We are spiritual beings living together. We have and are essentially removing your barriers to becoming a spiritual people. It with urgency that we tell you the earth will continue to crumble until more awareness has been achieved. No amount of magic or voodoo is going to change this. No amount of denial is going to change this. Emotional evaluation will change your view of spirituality, whatever that may be. Your love of life and others and also what is known in Eastern cultures will change the earth. Love, live, breathe."

We have included some of our own personal experiences and awareness in this book, but consider ourselves to primarily be conduits for information that has come to us through the healers. They told us to write this book and we are honored to deliver their message, which the world needs to hear.

Channeling this book has been an amazing process. Michelle and I (Jay) met at work, where we had a spiritual connection of sorts from the very beginning. Michelle approached me and told me that her brother (who had passed over) was prompting her to talk with me. She then asked questions to test the waters to see if my belief system was based in spiritual thinking.

So when Michelle and I started to write the book, we discovered that Michelle can channel and receive streams and blocks of information, while I predominantly receive ideas and concepts. Both of us received whole messages at times and at other times, it took both of us receiving parts to get an entire message. We would also incorporate feelings and emotions we received during channeling to allow us to accurately interpret the messages. We verified whether our interpretations were correct by asking the messengers if they were.

At times we would receive very large amounts of information and we spent many hours organizing it. Sometimes we would both receive information at the same time and other times we would receive it at different times. We live many miles apart, do not communicate daily and live very different lives. A lot of the information we would each receive separately on many occasions would be matching in content. We would meet and compare and say, "Wow!" We would know then that was pertinent information the messengers wanted in the book. It was and is amazing to us. We are both aware enough to be certain that what came through was from a light-filled, positive place and was for the greater good of all. Our guides would help us in this respect also.

It was and is a strange feeling when you suddenly have all these words, information, and directions in your head and there is an urgency to write or type them. We would have been thinking of other things (like being at work) and suddenly feel this urgent need to write down the information we would be receiving. We would write or type and not even know what we were putting down! We just kept going till we were done and could continue with what we had been doing. It would happen at our jobs, early in the morning, at night, at our homes, or while driving.

We met most weekends to have our writing sessions and we estimate we channeled 80-100 hours worth of information. We would end up with all these pages of notes, ask the messengers where they wanted us to put them, and we would be given the chapter numbers, so it at times was like putting a puzzle together. This was a very tiring process. We want to thank everyone, including our coworkers, who were so understanding and cooperative during this difficult time.

The messengers and healers who sent us the

information in this book have not only helped with writing it but have helped us increase our personal awareness. They tell us there are many helpers/guides involved in writing this book. Each contributes their expertise in different chapters and some in all the chapters of the book; it is a collaborative effort of many. We do not receive specific names and the messengers overall seem very humble in their contributions to the whole. They are all very positive, caring, and wish to express only love.

The messages we received revolve around a strong urgency to change our ways, starting now. They focus on becoming more spiritual, being kind to ourselves and others, saving the planet, blending Eastern and Western belief systems, and opening our eyes and being more aware of what is happening around us. We want this book to facilitate healing. Everyone chooses their own path in this lifetime; it is a matter of personal choice. Even though at times it seems we have no choice, we always have choices.

Throughout our lives, most of us ask God, the universe, or whoever our higher power is for help and we are given messages and choices. This is what the messengers have told us: We have made more bad choices than good; we have not heard or have refused to listen to the messages we have received; we have not had the awareness we need; we have not chosen paths that will lead to positive outcomes, and we have strayed from the spiritual path. Look at all the war, distrust, greed and fear, hunger and madness in the world.

INTRODUCTION

This book is about returning to a spiritual path and living from our higher selves. All of us have guides, angels, and helpers who present us with choices to achieve what we feel we need or want. When you leave the spiritual path or do not hear the messages and focus more on the ego, on cravings, on fear, and on greed, you do not serve yourself or the greater good of all. You dwell in negativity. You live in negativity.

Unfortunately, the world is out of balance. We need to return to the positive. And this is simpler than you think. We have not been aware enough to receive help from spiritual sources to keep us on a positive and kind path. We are told this book will make us more aware of the messages and choices that we get and it will help us to achieve balance. It will help you recognize why you are not aware. It has been written for everyone, regardless of religion, philosophy, or belief system.

If everyone lived with awareness and tried to maintain balance and respect towards the earth and each other, they would see we are really all one community. By picking up this book, it is a sign that you are actively seeking ways to simplify and improve your quality of life. You want to be part of the revolution of spirit that is happening. Please read the entire book.

One important step to achieving balance is to make choices that will enhance your awareness of your surroundings and environment. We ask that you make the choice to follow the path of kindness presented in this book. This book is especially for those of you who find yourselves saying, "I feel: out of sorts; not myself; not grounded; incomplete; or stuck." Do you find yourself doing something that you were not paying attention to and then saying, "What was I thinking?" or "What was I doing? I know better than that!" We hope this book introduces ways to counteract all the feelings of losing yourself. It is easy to be forgetful and lose track of being aware of what we have created around us and who we are. It is easy to lose track of how we live and how we treat each other with how we are trained, programmed, and influenced by the unrelenting barrage of marketing messages and disinformation we receive through every means of communication. It is easy to feel overwhelmed and lost trying to find explanations for the questions we have and the feelings that produced them with how busy the world has become.

We can break through the brainwashing that convinces us to be the best consumers we can be, to own more than we need, and to keep buying more and more. We can overcome the psychological programming that dampens our awareness of our actions and thoughts of ourselves and the earth and convinces us that we are all separate communities and not all one community. We are in this together, all of us. We have forgotten and been led away from remembering there were times and societies that successfully maintained community life, individual belief systems, individual rights, and balance with Mother Earth; societies with long histories. Everyone can benefit from remembering those times. We can blend the best of those times with the best of the present time. We must remember and realize again we can achieve anything we want to do or be.

We the authors are very happy with the message in this book and are very grateful we could be a part of it. We hope it helps you. Peace.

— Jay Hill and Michelle Kraus
2008

CHAPTER 1

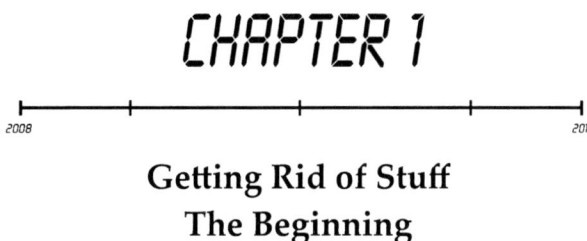

Getting Rid of Stuff
The Beginning

Once, human beings lived with very little of what they have now, but they lived with love and compassion and the will to survive. Do you still have that skill?

We live in a new world where we cannot continue to live as we have or use the earth as we have. Changes are coming, but anyone with a little perseverance and awareness can be prepared to embrace the coming world. Be prepared to be happy and to lose the trappings of domestication and the negative training society has ingrained in us. This is a book about returning to a place of love, hope, and balance;—not despair, fear, or disharmony.

We must return to a place where we get along with the earth and all its inhabitants. Things are going to get worse before they get better. Now is the time to prepare and be vigilant. Now is the time to be more aware of the surrounding world. Together with love, peace, and intent, and of course change, we can all live simply. We can live peacefully and environmentally friendly and still enjoy our advancements if we want to. But first we must return to a simple and emptier place and do it right this time. We do not want to repeat the negative parts of our history that include war, famine, plagues, and hate. We do not have to live that way. Let's start over together. It will be scary at times and hard to accept what we must do, but we must do something now. That is obvious or we will suffer and possibly not have a planet to live on.

It is simple. To begin, we start by just removing some of the stuff we own. We will then be able to breathe and see the forest through the trees. When you pass over, the love, light, and peace you carry will be what you will bring with you, not the material possessions you own. Do you really need all of those material things? What do those things provide? Do they really provide you with happiness? Does the time spent using those things bring you love and light? Be cautious and careful of what you wish for. This is our message to you.

Let's start with the definition of "stuff." Webster's Dictionary has several definitions for "stuff," including: "personal property, raw material, a finished textile fabric; writing, talk, or ideas of little value: TRASH; an unspecified material substance or aggregate of matter; (verb): to fill by packing things in; to eat greedily, gorge, to prepare by filling with a stuffing, to stop up/plug."

So obviously stuff is what we own, hoard, and keep for different reasons. As you can see and imagine, all of this stuff can block, stop up, and plug all of the energy flow of the good things in our lives, such as having time to laugh with our family or children, participating in our communities, and spending time with our neighbors. It can block the simple act of sharing.

Let's examine the stuff that we own. Look around you and what do you see? The average American family owns a couple or more television sets, multiple phones, multiple cars, and closets full of music, clothes, and toys for kids and adults. In the cities, we have houses and garages and rafters so full that we have to rent storage spaces. In the suburbs we have three to five thousand square-foot houses with three-car garages for single families to live in. Why do we need that much space or stuff? What happened to the awareness of the resources it takes to produce, maintain, and utilize that much space and stuff? We are taught to feel uncomfortable with emptiness in any size house. So by filling the house with stuff, we are taught that it will remove that feeling of being uncomfortable and the empty void we are told exists.

Look at all the people who are saying, "I am not happy"; "Something's missing"; "I don't feel right"; and "I am lonely." Some people literally say, "I feel there is a void in my life." They ask themselves what they should do. If we are unaware, the only answer we receive from all of the marketing in our world is to get more stuff to fill the void. The marketing tells us that we have these negative feelings because we don't have stuff. Is owning all of this stuff really making anyone feel any better? Does it make anyone feel more complete? Does it make a difference? Getting more stuff is not the answer.

Getting rid of stuff is the answer. Look at a child who has one or two favorite toys or that favorite blanket. Look at secular people who live simple lives in religious orders, or look at tribal people who live in very close communities. Look at some Eastern cultures. Look at people who are aware of how they live, how they treat the world, and what they want. In all of these examples they are reasonably happy people, the majority living without a lot of stuff and some with difficult lives. The big difference between most Americans and other cultures is the stuff that they own. The cultures and people we must emulate have very little and are happy with what they have. We have a lot of stuff and we are not happy.

Webster's Dictionary describes karma as, "the force generated by a person's actions held in Hinduism and Buddhism to perpetuate transmigration (reincarnation) and its ethical consequences to determine the nature of the person's next existence."

That definition speaks of some far ranging thought. We need to break it down and apply this concept of karma to our life and our time now on earth. So a good definition is what goes around, comes around. In our present system, we own and then discard and live in a disposable world. The karma of continuing to own and then discard and live in a disposable society is to live on a disposable planet. That does not work. We are being led away from remembering that karma exists. We no longer realize how many generations will be affected by what we do.

There are Native American tribes that have lived with the concept that the next seven generations will be affected by how they live now. Think about how you live now. In 2006, there were 50 billion plastic bottles for water produced in the United States. Thirty-two billion of those bottles ended up in landfills. We need to establish a system that takes into account karmic living in all areas. We need to be more accountable for what we are doing.

Society tells us from childhood that having stuff makes us better, hipper, cooler, and happier. They tell us it is necessary that we keep up with the Jones's to own better things and more of everything. The marketing people tell us that it is okay to live in a disposable society. Even people with little money are given the impression they don't need to respect or care about their stuff. We are told we do not need to worry because stuff is cheap and we can always buy more of it. Advertising is geared to these messages and we hear them from birth.

Look at what happens when there is any change in our lives, such as a birth, death, wedding, job change, or move, all of which involve getting rid of stuff. People get overly stressed. All of this is change and we are told that change is bad except the change of owning more stuff. These messages keep us from making good changes and keep us stressed. They keep us from trying to make any positive changes. When we are approached with change, what does marketing and advertising tell us? It tells us that when the going gets tough, the tough go shopping. The message is that buying more stuff will make everything all right and you will feel great. Some are realizing now that the first steps toward answering a question like "I feel like something is missing" is to live more spiritually, to be more aware of the marketing, to reduce the emotional attachment to all of that stuff and to get rid of it. But many, many more people on Earth need to do this.

We can still have what we need and we can still have stuff and be happy and contented. Successful societies throughout history that practiced sustainable living (and even the founders of the United States) understood how many resources were used to maintain unused spaces and take care of unused stuff. 'Sustainable' can be defined as using a resource (like land and soil) so that it is not depleted or permanently damaged, or living a lifestyle that uses sustainable methods. We can return to truly living, and living sustainably, with guidance from our higher selves.

With awareness you can recognize how much space you actually need to live and be happy. With awareness you can look at how much space you actually use and see how much stuff you have. But how can we be aware when all this stuff is in the way? We all have stuff that we have not used in years. Even though our stuff might be taken care of and stored in perfect order and out of sight, it is still clutter and stuff that we don't use. To build awareness of how much stuff we have only takes a little of our time. We first need to tell ourselves that we will take the time to deal with our stuff.

Now is the fun part. First instruct everyone in your household to make a list of what they would need to live and still maintain a modem of comfort and happiness. You will then see your expectations and the reality of what you think you need. Then make a list of everything that you own, down to the smallest things. Use recycled paper to write them down. These are the first steps to living more simply, becoming more aware, and becoming more spiritual. Make a list for every room. Don't forget sheds and garages and basements and rafters. Involve family and friends and make it a fun project. Maybe after making a list, cook dinner together. Eat together. Spend time together. Laugh together at all of the stuff that you own. After making a list of all that you own, again involve family and friends by having everyone mark what they have not used in a long time (a long time is more than two or three months; exclude seasonal items as they should have their own list). Try not to make this a chore. Try to make this a positive experience. It is not something that you need to rush or worry about.

Next comes the step that will be the most difficult. You must start making decisions about parting with the stuff that you don't use. Remember that you may be emotionally attached to a lot of it, so it will be hard to get rid of. For sentimental reasons, a lot of people even keep broken stuff. This is a time to involve your family and friends again and to make an honest and fair list of what you are going to part with. Look at the list of all of the stuff that you are going to get rid of and discuss with everyone if and how traumatic it will be to get rid of the items. Then everyone should discuss where you can go to get rid of the stuff and where it will have the most positive impact in the community that you live in. Try to personalize the experience by giving it to someone who you know really needs it. Discuss with everyone how what you are doing creates love and a feeling of community. This will be one of the greatest things your friends and family will learn and do together. This is the first step to freedom of spirit. This book will clarify why this is the path we all need to follow.

Now comes another fun step. Discuss how you are not going to buy into the marketing and get more stuff to replace the stuff that you gave away. People do not need to fill every empty space in their lives with stuff. Love should fill the empty spaces. It is okay to sell some of the stuff if you can just remember to stay positive and do something good with the money. Doing something good for yourself and others will help produce more positive karma and you can do this spending time with the ones that you love. If you find it difficult to figure out how to sell things or it feels wrong to you, remember it is okay to give the stuff away that you have not used or have no use for. The money you paid for it is gone and all this stuff is blocking the flow of love in your life. In giving the stuff away, please try to ensure that it is going to fulfill a need and that it is not just going to someone else who doesn't need it. Remember that to live responsibly, you need to fulfill your own needs without interfering with others fulfilling theirs. Do not block their love.

When you are in this project and nearing the finish line, the awareness of what you have created around you emotionally and physically will surprise everyone. One of the ways that you will be surprised is when you realize how all that extra stuff actually contributed to unhealthy competition, arguing, greed, envy, and unhappiness in your family. In keeping up with the Jones's, this thinking contributes to prejudices against your neighbors, other countries, other races, and other religions. Our present marketing system is international and does not contribute in any way to balance in our world or the international community; it is only there to produce a profit. Marketing does not contribute to any balance with Mother Earth. When discussing this with family and friends, talk about how much you own because advertising told you that you needed to have it. Most people do not even know how much stuff they own.

When industrialization started to pick up in the modern world, things changed. Prior to that time people lived a more simple life. There were no television sets, radios, billboards, signs, or constant advertising messages saying that we needed to own stuff. We were a society that was more focused on family, friends, and taking care of each other, and even though we were more survival-based, we lived in stronger communities. We did not worry so much about stuff. As industrialization increased, marketing became a staple of our society. The concept of training us to become consumers was born. Once we were able to mass produce stuff, advertising began to influence our lives.

Look where this has lead. It has lead to a disposable society that affects everything. We have disposable relationships, disposable families, and even disposable lives along with our disposable stuff. We buy more, use more, and want more, and we end up throwing away a lot of that stuff. We are now paying the price. Getting rid of stuff will break the strangle hold from advertising that controls the way that we live. Marketing has even marketed spirituality out of our lives and made it something separate. An example is that some churches have moved their services to Saturday night so that they would not interfere with football games broadcast on television. A football game is a great place to sell something to the tune of over $100,000 a minute to run an ad during the game.

It is so important that you clean out your stuff. It is the first step to being happier and in control of your life, and it will help you become more aware and make room for spirituality in your life. It is not a question of if we can break free from the marketing and the ownership of stuff, it is a question of what we have to do and who we can work together with and when are we going to start. Our world is dying, our gods are gone, our families are disintegrating (look at the divorce rate), and we sit here with all of this stuff. And we are continually told that we need more stuff.

Think about your spirituality, awareness, and community. Think about getting to know your neighbors. We need to know ourselves and each other and we need to know that we all effect our environment. We need to be aware and recognize how marketing affects us. We are not saying that we do not need to live without modern conveniences, without modern technology, or without advancing as a civilization. We are just trying to bring about awareness that we do not need to be led down our present path and that we can live with all our modern conveniences and still live in an earth friendly, people friendly, and more spiritual manner. We are a very learned society. But we can still learn from the past and different societies that were and are successful at sustainable living, and we can practice that way of life.

Being spiritual and being part of an extended family was and still is important to all happy and successful societies. We need to grasp these concepts and apply them the present. It is not a question of whether it can it be done—we know it can. We know it needs to be done. The question is what do we have to do and when will we start to work together on accomplishing peaceful living? We need to start making the choice of peace—peace with ourselves, peace with others, and peace with the planet. We need to see the choices and be aware that what we choose will affect our entire environment.

CHAPTER 1

What is the price you pay and the price your family pays for all of the work that you do to own all of your stuff? With multiple jobs, you really don't see your family much. You tell yourself that you are so busy that you cannot cook healthy foods. You are killing yourself and what you don't realize is that you are isolating yourself. Look at all the stress we are under. Some people have no work. Some have too much work. Some have no money. Some have too much money. We are going fast, fast, fast. We are never in the moment. We are going so fast we care only for the future. Whew! Slow down. When we do this to ourselves, we are not aware, we don't pay attention, and we harm Mother Earth. We have to make appointments to see family and friends. We have to make appointments to use all of the stuff that we own. We have to make appointments with our stuff. We are using our planet up. It is all connected.

We need to live in a society in which people and their relationship with each other and the earth are not negatively affected by changes in leadership or power bases. People and their families and communities are what counts, not stuff. It takes awareness and spirituality on our part to have such a society.

We are not saying that those with a lot are supposed to give up the abundance the universe has blessed them with, or that those with little must live without. We are saying: Look at how many resources you use and how much of your stuff you don't use; open your mind and eyes and look around you and see where things stand. If you have a lot to share, if you have little, live in the mindset that others will be sharing with you. The abundance the universe grants is for all of us. We ask you to respect what you have and respect what others have. Respect each other and live in peace.

Enjoy regaining your space, enjoy the peace and decreased stress that will come about when you clear the areas around you. Enjoy life. You can do it! Living simply is achievable and a goal that will give you immediate satisfaction, less stress, more time with family, and easier living. We are available to provide love, light, and peace if you ask us. Will you ask?

Now let's take a look at why you feel compelled to own all of that stuff and live the way that you live.

CHAPTER 2

Fear and Greed

We all have fear. Little fears or big fears, they all are fears. To defeat fear, one must look inward and find the original source of the problem.

What about greed? Webster's Dictionary defines greed as "selfish desire beyond reason." Look at society. We own. We buy. We store all of the stuff we are told we need. But what is it we actually need? How does need relate to greed? How does greed occur? Greed is when someone has more stuff than you and you want some of it. Greed is when someone has something particular that you want and you don't have the means to buy or own it through legal channels so you steal it. Greed means that you keep buying things and hoarding them because you feel all of that stuff will somehow make you more powerful and in control.

Look at what happens when things are taken away from people. They fear the loss of control and they have meltdowns, they panic, they go crazy, they sweat and yell and act crazy. They want the security that they have been told that their stuff will bring them. What people really seek is security from within, but they are not aware enough to realize this. How does one achieve security from within? By stripping away the elements that feed the ego. Fear and greed feed the ego. Marketing instills cravings and needs that then have the potential to become fear and greed. We must become more aware of ourselves and how we deal with all of these fears and greed.

Advertising connects fear with the need of a product through messages like: Buy this facial product at $900 or others will laugh at your wrinkles [that you received from the $75 monthly tanning booth package]. Other examples include the advertising to buy a certain name brand of clothing to look a certain way to be liked. Advertising also instills in us the need to have a certain size, color, or make of car, friends who live in a certain neighborhood or type of house, what kind of coffee to drink and on and on and on. You get the point.

At times what we will say in this chapter will sound extreme, but please bear with us. This book is about slowing down and being nice to ourselves after all is said and done. What is at stake? A lot. We are talking about not millions or billions but trillions of currency on a world scale. We are talking about groups that use the most advanced and diabolical methods to achieve a profit. They are the wizards of our time. They perform a magic that even they are even amazed at. What amazes them the most is after a time of testing and then implementation, the basic methods still get the same results they seek.

There are scientists and psychologists and marketing gurus who can tell you exactly how many repetitions it will take and in what order and in what duration of time to ingrain and train someone's mind and ego to believe exactly what they want you to. They use colors, sounds, graphics, and subliminal images to achieve their goals. They build programs into the marketing that will automatically make you rebel against anyone just saying that what they are trying to do cannot be done. They mislead and brainwash you to convince yourself that it is not happening and is not real. They have had access to the vast majority of people in this country and most parts of the world with seemingly unlimited time and money to do what they want.

Just ask yourself this: Why would perfectly sane people bankrupt themselves and put themselves in positions of working so much that they do not see and don't even really know there families? Why would they while in this position keep the same behaviors and go deeper and deeper into debt? We all know more than just one family like this and some of us are that family. Why would there be so much excitement about the building of and the growing of a middle class with spending power in China, India, and Mexico? With the building of these middle classes and all of their buying power, everyone knows it will tax the world's resources to a degree that will harm us all. Why are perfectly sane families of four living in homes they cannot afford and that are far too big for them? Why do some people need three of something (like four wheelers or snowmobiles) when they know they will never get around to using just one of the items and they already plan on getting the newest model?

Why do people keep doing these kinds of things over and over when they know it will burden them and their families, and it will hurt the earth? Everyone now knows that we are killing the planet, so why do we continue? Why do we seem to not care and only give these issues lip service and not make a greater effort to change? Because our culture believes that money is the most important thing in the world. We are cashing in our true happiness and our planet for the monetary gain of a few. And the few know what they are doing. One of the reasons there is a spiritual revolution going on right now is that for many people, they just cannot handle society's focus on money and buying and underlying messages.

Fear and greed is now a pervasive illness in society. It is showing up as war, hunger, depression, mental illness, addictions, divorce, crime, prisons, sickness, and now global warming, weather changes, and natural disasters. When emotion and fear and greed are tied together, the results are extreme.

Here are some examples of underlying messages that we receive from government, family, friends, and religion. These messages are delivered through print and electronic media and we are surrounded by these messages 24 hours a day. And if these seem extreme, remember what is at stake. We must realize that to sell things, the corporate world will go after whatever stirs the biggest fears, the most greed, and the most emotion in their ads. They use sex, death, and whatever else they can to accomplish their goals. People's lives are changed, children die, and the world has turned violent because people feel they have to have whatever they are being told to have to be accepted in the world.

If you don't have:

Money, the underlying messages you are given are: "You're nothing; You're a day late and a dollar short; You are a failure to yourself and your family; You need more, more, more and you can't legally get it if you don't have money; Something is wrong with you if you do not want money; You are an outcast and you are not good enough for anything."

Shelter, the underlying messages you are given are: "You need to own and if you don't, you are not participating in the American Dream; You need big houses with lots of rooms; You are sick or mentally ill or an addict of some sort if you do not have shelter or want shelter; You are an outcast and a failure."

A Car, the underlying messages you are given include: "If you don't have a car, you will never have a date and if you do have a date, how are you going to take him or her anywhere? Buses are for losers; How will you get to your job or see your friends or even have friends?; You will not be accepted by others if you don't have a car; You are a failure, and when you get a car or a nicer car, the better date, partner, friends, you will have, and you will be loved. Otherwise there will be only loneliness, fear and loathing."

A high credit rating, the underlying messages you are given are: "You will never be able to own anything in your entire life; you will be an outcast and a failure; You are a bum and no one will ever love you; You will be alone; Without it you are nothing; Even though you don't understand it and don't want it, you have to have it."

A partner/children/family, the underlying messages you are given are: "You are a freak if you don't want them and are not like the rest of the world; You must have mental problems or worse yet physical problems and you go against God."

Toys, the underlying messages you are given are: "No one will want to even be around you if you do not have boats, cars, snowmobiles, pools, campers, guns, four wheelers, etc.; There will be nothing to do if someone hangs around with you and you don't have these things; You will have no one and nothing to talk about or do; You are an outcast; You are going to be very lonely."

Drugs, the underlying messages you are given are: "You will die; You will be in pain; You will not live long enough to see your grandkids; You are sick not to want them; You will not be happy."

Television, computers, and media, the underlying messages you are given are: "You will never have anything to do without them; You will never know anything again, you will never hear any news, ever; No one will know you; You will have no friends; No one will find you interesting; You will be boring and a loser; If you don't own any of these things, you are sick, an outcast, and loneliness and fear and loathing will be with you forever."

Cell phones (this is a big one for teens), the underlying messages you are given are: "Sorry, you will have no life, friends, family, or communications; You will have and know nothing of the latest drama or gossip; That is the food of life you know; You are nothing because everyone in the entire world has one but you; You must be a freak, a loner, a sicko, an outcast, and everyone will know you don't have one; You must be a freak and have no sense of security; How will you ever be accepted if all of your friends have one and you don't?"

There is much more, of course, but we will not go on. It is sad and hurts us to see this happen when we are witness to so many losing their free will and losing the ability to make the proper choices that will help them learn the lessons they need to—lessons that will bring them closer to God, love, light, and universal energy; lessons that will make them more aware and thus happier. Knowledge is power and it leads to awareness, which is peace and growth.

There must be a return to a middle ground, a middle path, a place of no extremes, and a place of compromise. What happens to us is that through fear and greed we are lead to place of extreme emotion and action. When there is extreme emotion, that turns negative and the results carry over into all aspects of our lives. The extreme negative manifests itself as war, hate, prejudice, anger, illness, fighting, divorce, road rage, depression, and sadness. We need to open our eyes and we need to be aware and return to love, kindness, and forgiveness. We can change and not allow the influence of others to bring us to extremes. We can be sane and rational.

CHAPTER 3

Forgiving Yourself for Your Mistakes

Most people can see and understand the power of forgiveness. Forgiveness is part of love. Forgiveness is part of happiness. Forgiveness is part of acceptance. With forgiveness of self and others, we are shielded from all negativity and are free to love and take care of ourselves. We then can help others. Just think of the change forgiveness can bring if applied to world politics and world issues. Wow! No more war. Forgiveness will bring about just as much change in each and every one of us if it is applied at a personal level. Just imagine no more war with yourself over issues and emotions. No more disagreements with yourself. You need to start the forgiveness process at the personal level, and then extend it to your neighbors, then to the world. But you have to start by forgiving yourself.

Here is what we would like you to know. After you have worked with the ego and removed the stuff and become aware that you were greedy, then it is time to forgive yourself for feeling the need to buy, buy, buy and that what you have to have is better than your neighbors. Do not be afraid of the change that will come about in you when you no longer have the need for stuff. Take a deep breath and realize that what you have is adequate and be grateful for those things. Your family or your true friends will not judge or remove themselves from your life if you have fewer things or less stuff. Forgive yourself for wanting too much stuff and do not be afraid to change.

What do you know about yourself and how you will survive physical, mental, and spiritual change? Physically you will naturally adapt, but you will have to deal with mental and spiritual change at deeper levels. Some of the ways to help with change and awareness is to remember nature. Feel the wind and the grass and the trees and begin to absorb nature and the energy it provides. Feel the dirt and plant something and see how it grows. This is the road to increased awareness and forgiveness. You will be able to work through the issues and reasons for needing this stuff. Forgive yourself and move on to a more spiritual place.

You are human and you make mistakes and that is part of the reason you are on Earth. People make mistakes all the time and they still continue to exist. You don't need to be perfect. The change in you may occur over many years depending on what or whom you surround yourself with. But forgive yourself and you will change. If you are asking yourself if you were wrong or bad, that is not the issue or case. You are part of society and society tends to promote what is valuable at the time and that is what we learn. You must forgive yourself.

CHAPTER 3

We live in such a competitive and rushed society, things are being driven into our psyche all the time. We are constantly being told we need things. So it is so easy to fall prey to this programming, and beat ourselves up if and when we do not achieve the goals and possessions that we are told we need. If you believe all of the programming, it would seem we are not capable of thinking for ourselves. We are told that we can't be individuals who make our own choices and that we need all of this stuff and help. The human mind is a trainable and an easily led organ. The ego is easy to trick and have it do the work of training the mind. We can retrain our minds and egos for awareness and love. That starts with forgiving and loving yourself. We all have been exposed from birth to all this programming that is not about forgiveness and acceptance and love. Instead we have been programmed to be consumers and to do what we have been told to do. That is the path we have chosen as a society.

Let's look where this path has led. Our forefathers did not have all of the stuff we feel we need to have and they survived — the proof being we are here! We have different priorities and challenges than our forefathers had. We no longer need to work so much to survive. We no longer are close to nature and so we suffer from many disorders, among them seasonal affective disorder. We are freer to pursue likes and creative projects and art. We are freer to express who we are. But do we? The model that our present day society has chosen to follow seems to be more about letting others, negative aspects of our egos and group thinking about how our life should be dictate who we are and what we think we need, and who we think we want to be. And we are programmed the answers to the questions.

By keeping things too complicated, the sources of all the programming we receive keep us ignorant. There has been a promotion of separatism into groups. So it has become not only easy but it is encouraged to degrade, talk down to, criticize, and belittle ourselves and others. War in one form or another, from personal wars to wars with the world, is now the norm. Look at some of the most popular comedy in the United States. The most popular comedy belittles, makes fun of, and puts down other ethnic groups, countries, and religions; it has a very negative quality that is designed to shock people. It is good to laugh at ourselves but not others, but we have lost that distinction. And why do we have to be shocked just to laugh? Are we that numb? This has been the path chosen for us and by us at the present time. It is not working.

If the modern day psychological community had their way, they would diagnosis the majority of people with a mental illness. Look at the masses of the people going to healers, doctors, New Age and psychiatric counselors, and priests. These people seek help with emotional and spiritual issues, and issues with their relationships, families, and selves. Within whatever problem they believe they have, there seems to be a few basic themes that include the love and forgiveness of self, acceptance of self and others, and acceptance of situations. These themes come up over and over. When someone cannot do these things they do not feel part of themselves or the world. The common denominator of these issues is acceptance. Let us remember that forgiveness is part of acceptance.

> *"WHEN YOU FORGIVE YOURSELF,*
> *YOU CAN ACCEPT YOURSELF*
> *AND YOU CAN LOVE YOURSELF."*

There is a part of us that longs for acceptance, love, and happiness regardless of who we are or what we do or have. How can you ever let go and forgive yourself when you are told there is always something new, better, and necessary to have so you will be loved and accepted in the right crowd? What a message! We need to forgive ourselves for allowing all the programming and influencing to lead us to where we are. How can we even think about accepting ourselves or forgiving and loving ourselves with all the consumerism, and domestication by governments, corporations, and religions going on? Who are we?

The psychological community will tell you they feel 75 percent of all Americans could be diagnosed with some sort of mental illness. WOW. Look at how that labels people and the opportunities it creates for selling drugs. Now ask yourselves if this system is working. We are told how to act, think, dress, live, and even what to eat. No wonder we have anger and frustration, depression, confusion, and anxiety. No wonder we criticize and go to war with ourselves and everyone around us. By listening to all of these negative messages we have stopped thinking for ourselves, forgiving ourselves, and loving ourselves. We don't feel part of the whole. We are not saying that some do not need help with mental illness or that some do not benefit from the new wonder drugs that are available. But we feel the system has gotten out of control and so we are being affected adversely and it is not working.

We as a people need to start taking responsibility for what we create and do. That is a big step to healing and change: forgiveness on all levels. It is true that on a personal level, we can't really take care of anyone else if we can't take care of ourselves. This simple statement has been a way for many to see past a lot of things and to see more of just who they are. It has made many more aware of the decisions they make on a day to day basis that affects their lives. Why can't we love, forgive, and accept ourselves like we should? It sounds more complicated than it is. It is easy to not take responsibility for something we feel uncomfortable with and then to blame others instead. It is so easy to run with the group and not look at ourselves as individuals who can think for ourselves.

Let's take a look at marketing and how it affects society. Let's start with the exploitation of the desire to be different. In capitalism or socialism or any other "ism" (most especially consumerism), individuals can be made into a subgroup of the whole. Anyone who is part of a group (both adverse and mainstream)—rebels, free thinkers, bikers, health food enthusiasts, artists, hippies, doctors, lawyers, etc., becomes part of a demographic, and everything about them—their clothes, bikes, toys, cars, where they live, etc.—are chosen for them. They can be made to appear chic or not chic or anywhere in between. Anything connected with them will be marketable and there will be a monetary and an emotional price to pay. The hippy and then the grunge movements came along and suddenly holey and ragged looking jeans were on the market for $100. Academic people can be made to all look alike. If people can be grouped and categorized, they are manipulated and steered into how they should look, act, live, and even how they should talk.

Now let's touch on the wonderful world of guilt. For many around the world and here in the United States, guilt has been automatically built into our existence by religious dogma and doctrine and corporate and government habits of blame shifting, programming, and influence. We are told we are sinners, that we are evil, and that we are GUILTY—guilty of how our planet is being treated, guilty of how we treat ourselves, and guilty even of what past generations have done to other races and to the planet. We are made to feel guilty and ashamed because we have an average or bad credit score, because our house is not big or good enough, because our cars are not new or hip, and because we don't have every toy in the universe for our children or ourselves. We are told this over and over from birth and so we just automatically believe it and pass it down to our children.

On a subconscious level, we will always believe it until we become aware on a conscious level of what we are doing to ourselves and work to change it.

The truth is, we are not guilty of anything until we do something wrong. We are not at fault all the time like we are made to feel. We get manipulated and have the messages pounded over and over into our heads. We can change it, first by becoming aware that we are being influenced from the outside, which is more than half the battle. Then we need to recognize what is happening and what it is doing to us. Then we need to start forgiving ourselves for allowing it happen to us, and begin loving ourselves.

Let all the guilt go. We all are capable of this. Do not believe the messages you are getting from society and religions and government anymore. Cancel all the agreements you made with yourself to believe these messages. Then cancel all the messages you have sent yourself about guilt on a daily basis. Start giving yourselves new messages of love and forgiveness. Do this every day. With a little time, you will feel better about yourself like you should. You have been feeling guilty for a long time; be gentle and nice to yourself. Forgive yourself for allowing yourself to feel and live with all that guilt; forgive yourself for beating yourself up. No wonder we can't like or accept or be nice to ourselves. Don't even think that we do not feel all of the issues discussed here. We feel and are part of all of this. It's alright though; we can change ourselves and the world.

The current system that has instilled all this guilt in us is very unhealthy and does not work. It has failed and it is time for a change. This system has deadened our minds and awareness. It has kept us in line, unaware, and easily manipulated. Even the U.S. government seems unable to dislodge the lobbyists from its halls. Don't let negative situations drag you down. We can change, make up our own minds, forgive and love ourselves and everybody else. It can happen. Inside every one of us there is a part of us screaming and angry and confused and feeling like we are unworthy of love or forgiveness. Honor and listen and help that part of you. We can heal, together.

We are not saying that being in a group of people who have the same interests is bad or wrong, nor are we saying let's form another subgroup to be identified, labeled, and marketed to. We are saying that we can be aware of what we want, who we want to hang around with, and who we are without criticizing, chastising, and killing others for their affiliations. We can forgive ourselves and others for being steered down paths that are not our own.

Look how kids are killing themselves because they don't think they are being accepted or allowed in some group that over and over they are being told they need to be part of. They even kill each other over wearing the wrong colors. There are some who will kill to steal a pair of tennis shoes because they have to have them. We have to change or there will be more and more of the same. Wars, suicides, divorces, hunger, confusion, all result from negative programming and lack of awareness.

Change can come one person at a time, and that one can start to spread peace to a few more and so on and so on. We need to take the time, slow down, and start with whatever we can handle.

Turn off that television show or radio and think about your favorite people; stop watching the news, clear your thoughts, sit some place where you feel good, tell yourself you know you are a good person, forgive yourself for allowing others to dictate who you are. Tell yourself you love yourself and care about what happens to you. Laugh at yourself for being silly and doing some of the stuff you do. Remind yourself you need to be more aware and nicer to yourself. Remind yourself you need to talk to your partner and kids and friends about how and why you feel the way you feel (even the happy times); share. Ask them how they feel and how they are doing. You don't need to analyze your ego, learn deep meditation in a day, rush to enlightenment, see six therapists, take happy pills, or study the latest religion or philosophy. Keep it simple. Go for a slow walk to enjoy the movement and your surroundings. Or just find a nice place to sit. Do it alone or with someone else.

We don't need to constantly rush around. There is a commercial that shows a crowd of people in high speed buying fast with credit cards and then things stop because someone has cash, then everyone stares and looks down on and tries to make that person feel small because he has cash and slows down the line. The commercial is done in fast speed for a purpose: what a brainwashing tool for us and our children! Please do not believe that this does not have an impact on us. Millions of people see that commercial every day over and over. Don't be like that.

Just take it easy and try to step back and see some of the things you do because of others and the things we see like that commercial, and consistently tell yourself, "I am capable of making up my own mind, I am capable of change, change can be OK for me, I forgive myself and love myself and I like myself." Do this every day. Do it more than once a day. This is not complicated; don't believe it has to be. The more complicated others make things the more others are in control, and the less aware we are. Remember that inside of us all is someone who is angry and frustrated and mad because they know things are not right. We all beat ourselves up. Forgive yourself for doing that and start doing the opposite—love yourself. Beating ourselves up is part of how we are told to think and be. It is not OK, but it has happened and is happening; realize this and tell yourself you can change.

Remember, no one is perfect. And we need to remind ourselves of that sometimes many times during a bad day. Do the simple things in this book and that part of you will start to relax and slow down. You are emotionally and psychically sore and tired. It is a fast world you have been living in. You can be more complete and whole and happy. Accept yourself for the miracle that you are. You are worth it and at some level you know this. Allow that level to come forth.

You will find that when you can forgive yourself, you will be able to forgive others much more easily. Forgive yourself and others and others will forgive you. You will create a synergy of positive thought and response based on forgiveness. Each day we live in forgiveness, we create a past with a history of forgiveness. The karma of a past history of forgiveness is a future of forgiveness. All of this starts with forgiveness in this moment.

Forgiveness can be difficult but necessary. Keep it simple, be happy, and live in love and light. Once you have started to achieve forgiveness, then you can move on.

CHAPTER 4

Moving On

Now that you have cleared your space, seen how greed and fear have affected you, and forgiven yourself, it is time to move on. What does moving on mean?

Moving on is filling the space you have created with love, light, kindness, and peace. You do not need to involve any religious doctrine, dogma, philosophy, or spiritual path to see what comes from love, kindness, and peace. You will know if something comes from a place of peace if it holds no judgment, prejudice, threats, drama, negativity, or conditions attached to it. This basic tenant of truth that applies to all will always be simple and easy to understand. Most truths, like not killing or stealing, and living with compassion for yourself and others, apply to the basic truth to do onto others as you would have them do unto you. Live by these basic kind and loving truths that come from all over the world by moving on. Open your mind and you will see. Following these steps allows love into your life and then you can live from your higher self.

Let us use an analogy to discuss moving on in a spiritual manner. Let's say that your truck gets stuck in the mud or had a flat tire. You fix the tire, remove the mud, and move on with your day. Like the truck, before you can move on, you need to stop and realize that your true self is covered with mud and needs to be repaired. What that essentially means is that your true self has been covered with the mud and now it is time to wash it off with awareness.

So how do you remove the mud and enhance your spirituality and awareness? In this world of constant motion, it may seem difficult to do. It is really quite easy. Just slow down, breathe, and take in your environment, others, and yourself. Slow down, stop moving for awhile, and listen for the sounds of nature. Meditate and listen to your own rhythm of breathing. Taking the time to breathe will enhance your awareness, allowing you to become more spiritual.

Another way to enhance your awareness and spirituality is to cancel all agreements you have made with yourself to deal with emotional situations and life in a certain way. These agreements tie in with our upbringing, fears, wants, needs, and circumstances of life. These choices and agreements make up how we will deal with situations in our lives until we cancel them and make new ones. We start making these agreements with ourselves when we are small children. An example would be the child who is told not to sing because his voice does not sound strong or good to whoever is listening and discouraging him. The odds of that child singing for personal enjoyment for the rest of his life are very low. That child made an agreement with himself to believe whoever told him that his voice was bad.

Most of us do not even know what agreements we have made with ourselves. The faster the world goes, the less we see of these agreements. That is why we need awareness, slowing down, and breathing and introspection during times of meditation and prayer to see where we are at with ourselves. Like the analogy in this chapter, it is the awareness that we have or could get a flat and that our car needs to be cleaned but we thought if we pushed we could make it through the mud because we wanted to get to the donut shop or fast food place (after we saw that commercial on television) before it closed, and we didn't see the board with a nail in it then. We were going too fast. We did not take the time to slow down and be aware that we needed to take our time or the flat and mud would make us stop and cause us tremendous turmoil.

After you have slowed down, you can then let things go. You can examine whether you are forgiving yourself, loving yourself, and accepting yourself, and you can make sure you are not taking back any of the things you have let go. When things slow down, you can look at all the messages that you have been getting from everywhere and everyone and how they affect you, and then you can look at the messages you send yourself and the agreements you have made with yourself. You can see what you need to change. If you let go of things, you will feel a hole, because we are all trained that we cannot live with emptiness. That is wrong. We are never empty—we are always filled with love, light, forgiveness, and peace. We just get so busy and covered with mud that we don't see it.

Part of living spiritually and with awareness is realizing that we are human and need to learn some lessons about slowing down. Things happen for a reason. We can look at awareness sometimes as if we are trying to create this separate consciousness inside of us that watches what we are doing in our lives. Guess what? That separate consciousness is not separate. It's our spiritual side and it is part of us. It can help us when we see ourselves doing things that will bring us harm. Everything that happens to us in life can be watched, and we can get help with whatever we are struggling with.

Our spiritual side is not a stranger, it is our friend. It is the side of us that will help us to become more aware to recognize the guilt we put ourselves through. It will help us recognize how we beat ourselves up; it will help us realize how we are trained not to see our true selves or any other basic truths.

As stated in the last chapter, when all of this training and manipulation happens, there is no happiness; instead there is anger, war, and other problems. Look at the world around you. Look at how you feel when your neighbor starts mowing the lawn with a really loud lawnmower when you are trying to read or take a nap. In a situation like this, most of us become upset. We forget we all share the planet and are not separate. If we removed the emotion around us and our neighbor, and replaced it with love and forgiveness, we would barely notice the sound of the lawn mower. Or we would go over and ask nicely if they could do mow the lawn another time. They might say yes and then later come over and offer to mow our grass or replace that flat tire because they were fixing their flat tire and had their tools easily available. If they did those things, it would show that they had love in their hearts and it would also show you how karma works in everything. If you and your neighbor have forgiven each other for all the drama over time that you have been through with each other, life would be filled with peace, not turmoil. That is how life should be.

Moving on and being more aware is a matter of removing the judgment and assumptions and the training we received during our upbringing and from television and other media, religion, government, family, and friends. There has been too much programming telling us to believe that anything or anyone different should be looked upon differently and be judged. When we judge, we start to do that to ourselves. That is one of the things that we need to let go of. We are all who we are; we were created this way. What is wrong with accepting and loving who we and others are, no matter what shape, color, or size we are? You are you. You are someone to love. You are someone to care about. You are someone who can love and care about others. You accept yourself and you can accept others. We are miracles.

When living from your higher self, you will be able to tell after slowing down a little bit that you will start to move forward and be more aware. You will feel the positive energy around you. The easiest way to tell if you are moving forward is that you will be treating yourself, others, and the world better, and you will start to feel grateful for the simple things that you do have. We are told we need more of and bigger everything; all that does is take away from us the capacity to feel grateful for what we do have. It takes our perspective away. When we slow down, we can become more when we live more in the moment, when we just stop and breathe. We will be more grateful.

Look inside yourself and be grateful for the gift of life and who you are. Hug yourself and hug others you love. Tell them that you love them and are grateful for who they are. Tell them you are grateful that they were placed into the world to be with you, that you are grateful that they are here to help teach you life's lessons and also to be supportive, sometimes in ways you may not even be aware of. All of this is not complicated. Remember in the last chapter we mentioned that the world tries to complicate things in order to manipulate us? Life does not have to be complicated. We create our own environment. We can simply live, simply be, and simply love.

All of us need a certain amount of repetition to make change and help us remember things. Our short- and long-term memories require it. We are not perfect. Most of us don't have photographic memories. Most of what we have learned and absorbed has been influenced by the outside world and of course, by our emotions, fears, and who we are, and has been cemented in us by repetition. So it's simple to understand that it helps to create lists of physical things you need to remember but also mental lists of things you can do to reverse the programming. Write things down, ask others to remind you of things, keep forgiving yourself, keep loving yourself, and love yourself and others by withholding judgment. Instead of negative repetition, start doing positive affirmations and repetitions of loving behaviors. This is a simple thing to do.

When you make these lists and do positive affirmations, it is a good time to turn off any media, to just meditate a moment on who you are. This does not need to be a complicated process. You do not need to overanalyze yourself, label different parts of your ego, or figure out which archetypes are influencing every behavior in your life. You just need to say what you can do to slow down a little and watch a little closer how you are treating yourself and the world around you. Just think what a simple little list or note on the bathroom mirror can do. Have fun with it.

Another thing to do is to communicate more. Try to go out of your way a little more to communicate with neighbors, others you see and meet in your daily life, family, and friends. Let them honestly know how you feel and who you are. Do not talk about all your illnesses or how bad things are, talk about positive things. You will find the people who can help you clean that mud off or change that tire and you will be happier because they will be there to support you. We all need to do this. We can't keep letting others think for us. Look where it has gotten us in this world. We need positive support systems. Believe us, they are there. We just need to open our eyes, breathe, slow down, and gently look at ourselves in the mirror and the world. Look at who you deal with and you will see the ones you need to have around you; they will shine like headlights on a dark road when you have a flat tire and you know they are coming to help you.

Filling your lives with forgiveness, love, and kindness will help you become aware. It will help you to move on. You will see how you have treated yourself, the people around you, and Mother Earth. For yourselves and your children, look at what you are doing and leave them a place of wonder, love, and beauty.

CHAPTER 5

Returning to a Spiritual Community

As it stands, we are all in this together. We, from the other side, are within the change as well. We support you and guide you amongst all people in different lands each receiving these messages in their own way. Mother Earth is crying for our help and we come forward to help her. We focus on what is happening today with all people but know what will also happen in years to come. Replanting will help the earth, but rethinking will be a stronger modality for change. There are people who believe that everything will continue as is. That is the road they have chosen. Things will not be the same. There is help for you on your new journey.

This book has covered what you can do to clear out your physical, emotional, and spiritual self. It is here to help you live with more awareness, to live at a slower pace, to live with more peace and acceptance in your life, and to save you from the negative pattern you may have lived in. Now we will discuss saving and respecting Mother Earth. When people are more aware and balanced, they can create, manifest, and accomplish what needs to be done to reverse negative patterns. In essence, people can save themselves from turmoil.

When a group of people is aware and focused and works to promote peace and sustainable living, it can change society and save the earth. When enough people get involved, the energy will change the world. We need to create community; we need to get together with our family, friends, and neighbors. Talk with them about what you can all do to reverse and stop the destruction of the planet. We do not need to form a political or lobbying group, but a group of people doing something in their immediate environment to create change.

In a short span of years, the North Pole will be without ice for the first time in recorded history; it is happening now. For the children of the world to have a planet that can sustain them, we need to do something now. Let's look at common sense and see what is in front of our eyes. Scientists, governments, and historians can no longer look to the past to see and predict what our future holds. We are told daily what their predictions are, but look where listening to those predictions has gotten us. Our past did not have the technology that we have now, and the past did not move at the incredible speed of life we live at now. One year of air and water pollution combined with one year of rain forest destruction, the ravages of war and bombs, and the blatant disregard of resource use that we are now experiencing on a global scale is the equivalent of decades and sometimes centuries of global change in our past.

CHAPTER 5

Think of it—twenty-five years ago there were no computers, cell phones, or Internet in our homes. There were no GPS systems or smart bombs. Everything wasn't made of plastic. That's just the last twenty-five years, and it is amazing and sometimes scary to think of what the next twenty-five years will bring. We hear many predictions every day and the predictors even argue amongst themselves and point fingers at each other. Let's not worry about predictions so much anymore. We know things are bad and getting worse. We have talked about why we didn't see this coming.

One person, one small group at a time, can make a difference. Let's be more aware. When the Industrial Revolution started, there wasn't a lot of thought put toward population increase, sustainable use of resources, what harm we would do to the planet, or the overall psychological effects it would have on everyone. The powers of that time did not think about the situation globally. They dreamed of making money globally but the science, technology, and the logistics of the time were not conducive to that yet. They did not think about what would happen when one area of the earth had more technology than another, or what would happen when civilization reached the speed it has now. They did not think about what would happen when such an incredible amount of Earth's natural resources would be used up in so short a period of time. The thinking we now so critically need concerning small community living was left behind when we became a global world.

It seemed no one cared what would happen when the driving forces in our world became money and profit. We are now seeing what can result from those choices and it is happening faster every day. Our governments bow to the corporate world; whoever spends the most wins the elections, and war is now considered a profit producing venture. We are trashing the planet.

Let's be fair—it hasn't all been bad. Our technology has gone wild with advancement; our medical advances have jumped forward astronomically; most of us living in the Western world are wealthy by world standards. Considering the amount of food needed to feed our growing world population, our food is relatively safe. There are lots of positives but unfortunately, the time has come upon us where the negatives outweigh the positives.

We have approached the point of no return with destroying Mother Earth. Our leaders have not lived from their higher selves, and the lack of foresight and unawareness in our society has brought about changes that are harming us and the planet. Life has become way too fast. Global warming due to greenhouse gasses, war and the huge amount of resources used to support it, and the burgeoning population, has taxed the planet beyond its ability to support us into the future. In this chapter, we repeat a lot and will say again and again that we are fast approaching and in some areas have already arrived at a place of no return. We hear countless theories and studies, but it's time to just open our eyes and escape the fog we are in. The time for action is here. What has happened has happened, and now it is time to slow the process down and then reverse it. We need to take back control of our environment. Even if you do not fully agree with us on the degree and the urgency of what we say in this book, you can still open your eyes and see that a lot of what we say really is going on. The earth is ill and needs our love and help to survive.

We hope after reading this far that you have made a decision to make changes in your life. This is about individuals and community and our world. We are all one. Now is the time that we must bond together and help each other. We have allowed ourselves to be led from the good. We need to live in peace and to live sustainably. Those of us with gentleness and kindness must bring Mother Earth back to the beautiful life-filled, life giving being that she is. The earth needs our love to survive and needs us now. Who among you would not help a sick relative from becoming more ill and disabled without trying to help? It starts with one and grows into a community. So let us talk more about creating community. We need to break free from the cycle of closed thinking and domestication and allowing others to take care of us that we have bound ourselves to. Now it is time to share and start living a more simple life.

Our goal should be sustainable living in all its forms — to reduce our use of resources, to utilize alternative energy methods, and to grow some of our own food. We need to do these things in the big and small cities, the medium-sized and small towns everywhere. With our increased awareness, we must realize that there will be barriers in our journey, such as lack of space for gardening, lack of knowledgeable contacts and resources who can teach and help us, lack of reliable information, and of course financial concerns. But we must focus and remember that all barriers can be overcome. Remember that everything we will always need is here. Mother Earth will provide.

We have become too dependent upon others telling us our limitations and how to live. For example, let's look at lack of gardening space. The immediate reaction to such an issue is to slow or end your thinking process because of the lack of space. That is a conditioned and trained reaction. Instead, slow down and think of ways to make it happen. Perhaps you can create an herb garden indoors or seek neighbors who would be willing to share space in their gardens. Figure out how to connect with those who garden. Ask friends or family if they would be willing to share and lend a hand, or share the responsibility of maintaining a garden in exchange for produce. Educate yourself through conversation, visiting the library, doing research, and by exchanging books with others.

Ask the universe for answers to your questions if answers do not come easily. Quiet your mind and the answers will be presented to you; if not directly, then just be aware and watch, and you will be steered to someone who can answer your questions. We must increase our awareness of messages that we will be receiving. All the answers to your questions are out there waiting for you.

Be aware of coincidences that happen that may help you reach your goal.

Sustainable living really can save the planet. We need to restructure the way we are living so that instead of relying on the whole world to feed and sustain us, we rely on ourselves and our local communities. We need to be aware of how every thought and action we have affects us, our communities, and the world, because every action and every thought really does affect everything around us. Thoughts are the precursors to action, and every thought carries a vibrational frequency that really does affect everything around us.

Let us return to being small and self-sufficient, self-reliant, thinking for ourselves, and living as many small communities that make up the whole global community. Let's keep logistics manageable so that we aren't doing what we're doing now—using an incredible amount of resources to transport what we need to conduct our lives. The way we are living isn't working and it is harming our planet. Within a small group, you can keep the focus on what is important. Peace, sustainable living, and love, as in 'love thy neighbor' should be your most important goals now and into the future. Respect each other. We are all different in many ways but that does not mean we cannot work together. There is no politics in growing a garden together and sharing the abundance.

If someone tries to persuade and cajole and press their opinions on those of you who are trying to work together, let them know gently that this is not what your efforts are about. If they want to be politically active or preach a doctrine of any sort, there are plenty of other places in the world for that. Some will persist; just let them know that their opinions and beliefs are respected but perhaps your group is not the type of group they should be seeking. Ask them gently to go away.

People will get upset, but the focus of the human race must shift to peace and saving the planet. We have been taught extreme behaviors and drama and we must not pursue that course any longer. We can no longer afford to indulge in personal opinions or beliefs that keep us unfocused. Let us come together in these groups to eat better and cheaper, have less stress, save money, help the planet, and live in peace sharing things. Keep it simple.

There are many fun and fulfilling ways to start the process of returning to the earth. We should start by talking to our family, friends, and neighbors. For some this will be out of their comfort zone. In some cities and areas you might not know your neighbors; go for it anyway. Remember to focus on your own neighborhood. Avoid the pattern of thinking more, more, bigger, bigger. Slow down and start small. Remember, this is not a group that will be used as a business or a political tool. It is not a religious vehicle or a profit-based entity. We want to create, in essence, small nonprofit, self-sustaining communities; small societies that you and others in your group involve yourselves in to promote peace, kindness, and self reliance. We need to break away from thinking of ourselves as separate from our neighbors and create new lifestyles in which we rely on each other for love, support, and nourishment.

Even if you start small with two or three households to create a community of this kind, others in your neighborhood will notice that those of you who are participating are not as affected by things like inflation and recession. In your communications with neighbors, see who is interested in supplementing their food supplies and other needed items for little money, trading, or bartering. Start groups that teach people about gardening or lowering household expenses. Create newsletters about saving money and sharing, accepting diversity, kindness, and spirituality; get together to meditate, drum, swap child care, or can food. Honor everyone who does and does not participate; respect their views and opinions regardless of their background, circumstances, or situation. You will have less stress and be happier. You will supplement food and household expense budgets. You will save money. Others will see this and want to be part of it. If something is meant to grow big, it will, so relax and enjoy the journey. All things, if left to their natural path, will grow to the size they need to be.

Our term for this silent revolution is the Living Simply Movement. The three predominant areas of the movement's focus are peace, sustainable living, and awareness, not necessarily in that order. These three do not need to be nor should they be attached to any doctrine or dogma, or any large organized group. Keep it simple.

Individuals can and will go beyond what any group is doing, but focusing on those three areas within any neighborhood group will keep everyone busy enough. Be aware and you will know when you have reached the perfect size for your group.

Living simply—step by step

To connect with your neighbors, start by putting up signs on telephone poles and wherever you can (but not on trees) that ask people if they want to reduce their food bills by growing their own food, save money on child care and home repairs, ride share, etc. You will be pleasantly surprised at the response. We are all in the same boat. It does not matter how much money or how much stuff someone owns, or how well off they are, we all can use help. We all want to do these things. Remember to just keep the group to a small neighborhood group. If you get a large number of replies to your signs, then someone should volunteer to organize all of the responses into geographical neighborhood groups. Everyone will be able to share and barter. So do not worry if the group seems small.

Here are some things to discuss / activities you can do within your neighborhood group:

Grow your own food

Get together with people who are like minded. Create a team and decide who will be growing a certain crop and estimate how much of that crop would be needed to supplement the households in your group. Add up the numbers for six months, then one year using your current resources. If no lot or gardening area is available to grow food, use clay or small container or pots and start with herbs or tomato plants. Something to consider while planning is who will take care of the plants if someone is gone.

Think about what you need to do to be able to sustain enough food for the entire group without having to make large purchases from the store. If an area is available, try planting potatoes, corn, peas, green beans, or whatever you want to grow, but rotate the crops by growing different plants in the same places each year so that the soil doesn't become depleted. Plant one or two crops to each person who participates and try to keep them growing and continually producing enough food for your group.

As you get going you can increase the size of your garden and then challenge yourselves to be sustainable during the winter months. Discuss how you will collect and store your food during the winter months using modern conveniences like food dehydrators. Talk about canning and freezing food and making stews and soups to extend the life of your vegetables. Talk about where the food can be stored and how it can be stored safely among the group if everyone does not have enough storage or freezer space. Talk about how the food will be distributed and how often. These discussions promote communications within your miniature society. Other things to consider include:

- Will there be a coordinator for the group?
- How will you account for and deal with drought?
- Too much water?
- How will you store water?
- How will you calculate the number of plants grown, taking into account extra food that will be needed for holidays, celebrations, and family members visiting from other areas?

Your challenge will be how your group will sustain your standard of living without going hungry, being greedy, hoarding, or going broke. This may seem complicated and overwhelming, but it is not. People have been doing this for centuries. This can work. Get your hands dirty, feel the energy of the earth and the miracle of life. We can provide for ourselves with organically grown food and become healthier beings. There is something very satisfying about eating the food we grow because we can appreciate all of the time and work that was put into making a plant grow and produce.

Share the childcare

Get to know your neighbors and share the load. Daycare is very expensive. If there are retired or semi-retired people in your neighborhood, or stay at home parents, or single parents, discuss with them if they will help in exchange for food, work around the house, or rides. Sharing rides is very important. There are too many one-person car trips in our society. Think about how much money your group could save per month sharing rides.

Make and sell things and sell stuff

See who in your group wants to organize making or collecting blankets, quilts, clothes, household items, etc. Everyone needs all of these things at one time or another. They are great to share. See who wants to have a garage sale to raise money for other group projects like community bikes, scooters, or vehicles.

Save energy

Figure out ways to produce your own energy or raise money to obtain alternative energy sources like solar or wind or new technologies. We all have to cut down on our use of fossil fuels. Fossil fuels are a major contributor to the pollution that causes global warming. Start by encouraging everyone to turn off lights and stop using as much electricity as they can, because electricity is a major source of pollution and global warming, but the goal is to become self-reliant using alternative energy sources. You might start with just one household in the group and work to make it more efficient. Then add one house at a time until every house is involved.

Share/barter for mechanical work and other repairs

Find out who in your group can fix cars, do carpentry or plumbing, or just general handyman work. Get them involved in the group doing something they like to do.

Think of the money, time, and headache you could save if everyone in your group implemented all of these activities, which not only have monetary and physical benefits but also help the earth. It is a win-win situation.

In chapter seven, we will talk about the global effects of the small community group. Remember, this is a guide; it is not the be all and end all of how to accomplish what you want. It is just a guide to help you on your journey to living more simply and sustainably and in a more earth friendly and peaceful manner. This is also a guide to bring us together to get through the coming troubled times. Human imagination and ingenuity will help this whole process to succeed. Relax. Live, love, and breathe.

CHAPTER 6

The Path of Peace

In dealing with community, we cannot emphasize the power of getting along enough. The world is drowning in a sea of negativity. The negativity is created by prejudice, hate, and separation. If we are going to save this planet, help save each other, and help ourselves, it is imperative and necessary that we start to get along now. It does not matter what color we are, what our background is, or anything else—if we don't get along, we will no longer exist.

In the last chapter we talked about how we can physically affect our environment to help save the earth and ourselves. We will now discuss the emotional and spiritual aspects of survival. The key to these is getting along with ourselves and each other. With the extreme emotional programming we have received, we have been put in a position of taking sides. We live in an unhealthy competitive society not of our personal making that pits one religion against another religion, one color against another color, the young against the old, this area against that area, this team against that team, us against them, you against me. It has gotten out of hand. We are all of the same energy so we need to see that there are no differences between us. The more we become aware and spiritual the more we can counteract the differences and the separation they create. We can then walk the path of peace together.

As we conduct our daily business in the world, we talk to all kinds of people; some we feel comfortable with and others we don't. Why is that? Because we have made a connection on some level. The connection may be the same belief system, the same look or style, the same angels watching over us, the same vibration level, or perhaps we already connected in a previous life. Whatever the connection, it is a connection of energy of some sort. Wherever it is based or whatever you believe is not the point. What is important is that the journey toward those connections should result in being positive. During any interaction that we have, we must try to be aware and understand why the connection occurred. Sometimes it is just a trivial thing but the majority of the time it is not. What we need to do is try to figure out why we accidentally bump into someone with our grocery carts, or why we seemed to meet that person in that moment. We get help all the time and we need to be more aware that the circumstance is not just a coincidence; there is a reason for everything. We need to connect to others with meaning.

Science has found that we make decisions within the first fifteen seconds of any interaction with someone that will effect how we will be dealing with that person throughout our relationship with them. In these few seconds, we will either feel a connection or a resistance to that person or persons. We will decide if we want to pursue the connection or we will not. We will know if they are someone who we can help or if they can help us. This is where slowing down and being aware helps; it is living intuitively. The awareness starts with a conversation, a comment, a smile, a compliment, or a frown. For example, most of us make a connection to babies that smile at us and we positively respond and communicate by making gah-gah noises. We feel happy and good. A baby does not have the programming and training and domestication that we as adults do. So it is a very spiritual connection, from sprit to sprit.

We all feel good the instant that we connect with someone who is on a spiritual path also. Does it not seem easy to speak with holy people from whatever belief system they are from? On the other side of the coin you may feel resistance to the person who you sense a negative feeling about. For example the angry driver who will, at the risk of all, make very poor judgments on the road that could hurt many people. We in turn get angry and cuss them out. Because many of us have been programmed to react in an extreme manner, we react negatively to these types of situations and compound the problem. When we feel resistance or negative emotion, we do not need to react likewise. That is not a path of peace. If you are not aware of what your emotions are and you are not living in the moment, then you are going too fast. Please slow down and you will notice your environment and your reactions and emotions in situations. We all need to try to increase our awareness every time we are in a community setting. Becoming aware and communicating positively does not have to be complicated. It can be very simple. It will help us get along.

We all make choices in everything we do. We can choose a path of peace or we can choose a path of turmoil. The choices we make every day are affected by who we are and the outside influences of our life and our upbringing. So when we become more aware of the choices we have made, we can see how we are really dealing with others and the earth. We can then work to change. Slow down to better see the choices you make.

In Eastern thought, the thinking of awareness is incorporated into everyday life. There is no reason why we cannot apply that way of thinking to our Western way of life. Slowing down, being more aware and living simply is not going backwards. We should be able to live with more passion and enjoy every aspect of our lives. When we are aware of how we face and deal with the world, we can face and deal with all relationships in a more positive manner in our lives. We need to improve the relationships in our lives with ourselves and others. We then can work toward improving the relationship we have with the earth and each other so that we can live in peace.

It is time to create a community where everyone bases

thinking, doing, and being around love and peace. In the context this book, we keep talking about living on a path of peace. We speak of living for the greater good of all. When you live from a place of peace, you live without judgment. You live with humility. For a definition of humility we would like to add this one from Carlos Castaneda's book, The Circle of Power: "Humility is not to lower your eyes to anyone and at the same time not allow anyone to lower their eyes to you." In other words, we are all equals. Mother Earth is our equal also and should be treated with the same respect. We should all be in a state of peaceful togetherness, with each other and with Mother Earth.

As we have mentioned, we need to blend Eastern and Western belief systems. This blending was mentioned in Shakti Gawain's book, Living in the Light, in which she states, "The energy in the west (Europe and United States) is more masculine. It has focused primarily on developing the physical realm while paying little attention to spiritual development. As a result, we have made incredible technological progress but we are experiencing a terrible poverty of spirit. A feeling of disconnection from our source."

Let's get back to our source. Let's take that path of peace and think for ourselves again. Let's stop letting marketing influence us so much and leave some of the material thinking behind. Let's return to thinking spiritual and living from our higher selves.

We all need to put aside assumptions and hearsay and ignorance about Eastern thought or any thinking or beliefs that are different than our own. A path of peace is about gaining knowledge and wisdom and using that knowledge and wisdom as a guide to self realization, compassion, and healthy change. Eastern beliefs call self-realization and the wisdom you get from it, awareness. The world is changing and Eastern thought is already emerging in Western culture, we just need to be aware of how it has influenced us and cultivate a greater awareness. Even the Western medical field will acknowledge the benefits of awareness and the tools to achieve it, such as meditation, Qi Kong, and Tai Chi. To follow a path of peace, slow down and lift the veil of ignorance that has kept you from seeing what is happening around and within you, no matter your beliefs or non-beliefs.

Here are some examples of Eastern wisdom that are non-secular and can a have huge impact on individuals and community. The Eastern way of thought is full of wisdom. Wisdom consists of laws of nature and physics. Wisdom is truth that applies to everything but is not attached to any system or dogma. An Eastern wisdom that applies to our message is karma, which is the truth of cause and effect. Buddhists speak of karma a lot and it is a moment-to-moment part of Buddhist life that teaches living correctly. Buddhists use the term, 'Dependent Origination,' which means that every cause has an effect and every effect has a cause. What is happening around us is dependent on how we act.

CHAPTER 6

In Awakening the Buddha Within, author Lama Surya Das writes about karma. He says, "Each of us is a composite of different experiences, a whirling, changing congeries of conflicting forces and habits. Some of these experiences are in our memory banks; some are in our body; some are like knots, kinks, and twists in our energy." He goes onto explain that some of these experiences happened last week, while others may, according to Buddhist belief, have happened a hundred years ago. Each experience impacts us and leaves us with a karmic imprint that conditions us with reactions and responses to additional experiences. It is easy to see the cause and effect he describes and it makes total sense in many areas of our lives—"What goes around comes around." This saying covers things on a personal level and from there it is easy to carry it to a global level and see how what we have done and are doing has and is affecting the planet and weather.

Remember the lyrics from the old Beatles song, "Instant Karma": "Instant karma's gonna get you, it will knock you off your feet"? Well, we are being knocked off our feet by the karma that the present system has created. What we do causes new karma all the time—positive produces positive and negative produces negative. We have to start changing the karma of the world right now or our children will not have a world.

The Buddhists also speak of "The Three Poisons"—those things that blind us from what is happening around us and are the source of all suffering. They are anger (rage and wrath), greed, and ignorance. We have spoken over and over in this book of these things. In the West, we live in an angry world, not by our personal choice. We are surrounded by greed, and we are kept ignorant. A blending of ideas from East and West will help end the suffering that has been caused by these poisons.

Jay [one of this book's authors] has a friend who has spent a lot of time in Bangkok, Thailand and to this day is so amazed that there is no road rage there even though traffic there is much worse than it is in the United States. That is a very strong point and shows that simple concepts and wisdom can be practiced on a culture-wide basis in a society and have a positive effect. Just think of the blending of the good from East and West and how it would create an energy powerful enough to not only save the earth but make it better for many, many generations to come.

Another concept in Eastern thought that applies is duality, a term that refers to how we see ourselves as separate from all other things. In this separateness we desire or are repulsed by all things separate. We then divide the world into subject and object, me and everything else. We then continuously grasp for things we think are separate from ourselves to try to make us happy and whole. But nothing seems to ever satisfy us for long. Does that ring a bell concerning Western marketing? All of these points are easy to relate to and understand.

There is much more wisdom and many other points that will get the wheels in your mind turning. You should find out more for yourself by reading a couple books and discussing them with friends. Discuss it in your neighborhood group. If any concept or information upsets you because it sounds different than your personal religious or philosophical beliefs, then get something that explains a common wisdom of Eastern thought or ask your clergy person for some suggested reading. The odds are that in their theological teachings, they had to read something similar to what you are interested in learning. Please do not close your mind off to other ideas, because that is one of the problems that has gotten us into the mess the planet is in. Remember, we are all living souls living together on a living planet and we are all neighbors who can all be friends.

Part of Eastern thought is living rightfully and one of the translations of that into Western ways is to live responsibly. A good definition of responsibility is fulfilling your own needs without stopping any others from fulfilling theirs. This can be applied in so many ways; for example, people pushing their belief systems onto each other or using money to gain power to create change that only they want; or nations using too many natural resources or preventing a natural progression of growth in other societies. We need to return to living responsibly and from our higher selves and include Mother Earth in everything we do. Buddhists try to live rightfully by being compassionate in everything that they do, from their jobs to how they treat themselves and others. With even a small beginning of awareness, one can live more compassionately.

The present Dalai Lama said, "Compassion is not religious business, it is human business, it is not a luxury, it is essential for our own peace and mental stability, it is essential for human survival." Making the simple choice of peace over turmoil in whatever decisions you have to make during the day will help you in acquiring the mental stability and survival the Dalai Lama speaks of.

Another idea from Eastern wisdom that is hard for some of us to grasp is that craving causes suffering. In other words, if we stopped craving whatever it is we're obsessing about, and stopped responding to negative marketing, and stopped believing we need something and need it right now, we would became more aware. We would see how those thoughts make us feel inadequate because we do not have all that we are told we need, and we would get in touch with our true selves. We would not feel bad and suffer over the negative emotions that are stirred up.

What we mean by "true self" is being who we are without all the programming and negative marketing. Our true selves will always choose a path of peace. So try to recognize any cravings that were caused by outside influences and if it appears the cravings could be harmful in any way, and change your behavior to prevent it from affecting you negatively. An obvious example of a craving and marketing working together is a big juicy burger advertised over and over on television. That craving that is created is something that could lead to a path of turmoil such as in obesity, diabetes, and ill health. In the United States people eat overly large meals and keep eating way after they are full; they also eat way too many fatty foods. The marketing and training has influenced our choices and awareness of what and how much we eat and obesity is a visual result. The craving produced by the marketing has influenced us as a culture and is leading us down a path of turmoil and not a path of peace. It's okay to have a burger, but not okay because you are giving in to marketing; you probably were not even hungry.

All the points just presented from Eastern thought can be used to make our lives better. An Eastern saying is, "there are many boats on the river." This means that we are all different but heading in the same direction, carried by the current of life. We are all in this together and the start of any journey is just one step. Let us get together to take that first step together and start the journey down the path of peace.

So whatever dogma, philosophy, or belief system you abide by is OK, just try to be more aware and keep your mind open. Be aware that there is no special place or building needed to make choices and be peaceful and get along. Start in your home and be kind to those who live with you. Or if you live alone, be kind to yourself and your neighbors. Be kind to the person in the convenience store who seems to be in a grumpy mood every time you visit the store. Maybe some day that person will return some of your kindness. Take the path of peace when on the highway. Let that person who is in such a big hurry to get that one car length ahead of you in to the place in front of you. It's safer for all that way. Make the choice to slow down so that you can be more aware of your environment and the path you travel. We create our own environment, so create an environment of peace. We need to stop going to war with each other. Stop killing the planet. We can make this change. Start by taking a deep breath and begin your journey to increased awareness and living simply and getting along. You will need to remember that when you begin your path of peace, you must first begin to love yourself, then others. Simply live; live to simplify.

Buddhists exchange thoughts and conversation and understand differences rather than reacting to the differences. Reaction is not awareness. When your beliefs are different from others', reaction to what others have been telling you, how you've been told you should feel, and to the need to fit into society, your community, and family causes more criticisms and rejection. Reduce the rejection and replace it with love and understanding. Barriers to communication and to understanding the differences of all cultures fall away from the psyche when the path of peace is followed.

You can still follow Buddhist ways without being Buddhist. What we fail to understand is reaching for those in need with love; when they are helped, their good karmic choice is to return the love to someone else.

It's like balancing the water and food in your body— you need a balance of each to function as a whole, healthy being. When one part of your body is out of balance, it affects the other parts of your body.

If one portion of the earth is out of balance, then other parts of the world are affected by the imbalance. If one place has more food than what is needed, other places will have none. What the earth and its people are missing is balance—spiritual, mental, and physical balance. People continue and will continue to be confused about where they fit into the world because they are out of balance. Part of regaining balance is through choosing a path of peace with others; then when anger and all those negative emotions have relaxed, then begin to fill and replace the empty, unbalanced portion of yourself with the spirituality of love and compassion. Using the elements of Buddhism, we begin to be more whole, and to be one with the earth and each other, thus promoting togetherness and whole. The flow of energy on Earth will be significantly different when large amounts of people begin to realize that they can make a difference with the choices they make.

CHAPTER 7

Dealing with Society

In science, heat is energy, so it is obvious that with global warming occurring, there is a shift in energy that is planet-wide. There is also a spiritual change happening planet-wide.

There is an energy shift coming our way that will be huge, since the balance of so many things on the planet has been upset. It will affect people, animals, weather, the seas, and land masses. It has already. So we must be physically and emotionally prepared to deal with what is happening. Take it upon yourself to study the subject of energy shifts and the effects they have on the earth and people, and share the information with others.

The intent of this book is to help in forming energy that will radiate out from all people who will and are working for positive change. Thought is energy. Intent is energy. Everything is energy. Energy creates our environment. It creates happiness and sadness; it creates all and is everything.

The goal of humanity should be the production of a wave of positive, sustainable, happy energy. That is what will change the earth. Everything changes all the time; change is constant. As a people, we need to stop using our energy to fight change and instead go with the change. We need to steer the change to a better place with our behaviors.

Everyone needs to say no to the present system. We need to turn away regardless of any fear or resistance. Fear is the tool of resistance—fear others will have more control; fear that there will be an increase in the price of basic items; fear of increased chaos; fear of feeling different because of energy shifts and changes; fear of feeling lost and not sure what to do; and fear of the loss of jobs and an identity and place in the world. Plants and animals will be affected just as much as people when the coming energy shifts arrives, and like people, some of them will go crazy. Everyone will and does have resistance because they fear these things, but people must return to a place of having faith that they can deal with these things and everything will be okay.

We must think for ourselves. If we change our thought patterns, we will change the energy, and worldwide plants and crops will be plentiful and affordable. Change the energy to being positive and full of light and love and the crops and oxygen-giving plants worldwide will be able to feed everyone the food they need and provide the air they need to continue to live. There will be less hungry people if everyone would work with the earth and be thankful for the dirt and the rain that the heavens have provided to grow food in the earth. Being thankful really can change the energy.

Energy starts out heavy when filled with resistance. As resistance increases as it is doing now, you will need to step back and increase your awareness of the shift. This is when you will need to reorganize and start fresh. You need to be ready.

When will this occur? It has already started. People are becoming more aware, as evidenced by increased community events, more people using bicycles, and books like this one being published. More needs to happen. More people need to start thinking for themselves and taking back control of their lives.

Most people are sick and tired of making their life decisions based on money. Money controls everyone in almost every aspect of their lives. Money determines what size house we live in; what type of car we drive or what kind of bike we ride; what brand of food we buy and what type of clothing and friends we have. Why should money have anything to do with the people we know and want to be around? What if the person you will be most compatible with lives in a lower income or higher income area? Society will pressure people to think that they need to stay in their own geographic area and only interact with people who have similar interests. Should we be basing how we interact with others based on money?

It is time we start losing our resistance to change. This can be done without going to war or damaging the earth. We must all try to send love and understanding to others around us. The messengers have some to us again and again to say that they are ready to assist in providing a way of light and love and peace. Your spiritual guides and guardian angels are there for you too. Use them as a resource to help you to increase your awareness of your environment and emotions and how they are associated with your everyday situations.

For example, if someone in your office or your neighborhood rubs you the wrong way every time that you see them, step back and look at the emotion. Ask yourself why you are experiencing that emotion. Are you part of creating that environment? Then ask yourself what the path of peace would be in dealing with someone who is constantly in that state of mind. Try to recognize if you keep yourself in the same state of mind. Acknowledge their emotion and provide support and understanding in a kind and loving way. This acknowledgment may increase the other person's awareness. Maybe they weren't even aware that they were presenting themselves in that manner to begin with. It may be difficult to do this at times because it goes against many things that people are taught.

Do you sometimes think, "What's wrong with that guy?" Or, "Why is she so crabby?" Instead of thinking like that, take a chance and be empathic with their emotion; ask them what's bothering them. Maybe they only need that one little loving question or comment to increase their awareness of how they may be acting. Then ask yourself why you reacted the way you did. Take the time to slow down and talk about it with them. When you know someone even a little bit better, it is easier to start spreading peace. When people start to get along and share and work together, that is the time to start bringing increased awareness and a message of peace and healing to the corporate world and governments and individuals who are damaging the earth. They probably already know who they are and what they are doing, but they will need to hear many, many strong voices to change their behaviors.

In creating change within society at large, you first start with making the changes we have discussed individually and in small groups. You start to record the changes you have made and how you are achieving sustainable living; record how you are reducing your cost of living, and then show this information to other people and leaders living in your area. The people you show the information to will take notice. The leaders themselves must be personally impacted by the need to change or they will continue with their way of life and not recognize the efforts of those who want to respect the earth.

How long will it be before the money, goods, food, and water runs out and no one can exist independently? With the changes that are coming world-wide as we head toward 2012, this is happening faster than we all think, and parts of the energy shift have already begun. The road we speak of will be rocky, but it must be taken. As history has shown, the most influential and memorable people in the past had minimal belongings. Jesus, Gandhi, the Buddha, Mother Theresa, and others like them had very little but they worked toward a better world. To some degree all people must emulate leaders such as these. We must not follow present day leaders who allow the wealthiest to persuade us to live a certain way, to live in chaos, and to knowingly allow consumerism to continue at a pace that is increasingly more damaging to the earth. Companies, governments, and individuals who try to control people and who are damaging the planet need to be shown that people are paying attention to what they are doing. They need to be shown that people are now paying attention to profit margins and yearly profits and what the true cost of achieving that profit is.

What can you do to reduce your reliance on those who harm the earth and base their decisions on money? Don't support their cause. Turn away. Start using alternative energy like solar panels, windmills, and public transportation. Start using the earth to grow your own food to reduce the profit margin and sales of these entities and see what happens.

Ask yourself if you really need to buy a newspaper every week that results in the destruction of acres of trees, and whether the information in the paper is vital to your existence or if it is drama that may cause confusion and chaos. If you must have a newspaper, ask the newspaper company providing it if the paper used can be provided in an earth friendly manner. Do the same with the companies that send an unending stream of coupons into your house each week.

People need to let leaders in all realms know they are asking these questions. We understand it will be difficult to turn away from the present system in even small ways. But we must do something. Throughout this book we have pointed out most of the reasons why it will be difficult to change. But our greatest hope is to leave the old ways of doing things behind. We cannot keep beating our collective heads against the wall trying to make a system work that is not working.

We can pull back from the insanity of the present system and use technology and science and still turn away. We can turn away in a manner that is not vindictive or angry but just a return to a focus on us as a people, on our families and values, and on what we as individuals can do for the environment and each other. Everything starts on a personal level and on the level of the immediate environment we create around us. We can slow down and stop participating in negative cycles and do this without abandoning society.

We cannot emphasize the urgency of what we are saying enough. Please do not look at what we are telling you as turning your back on others. By turning away from greed, by healing the planet, and by working with others and spreading peace, you are not throwing away your life. You are not running away from anything. You are moving forward to taking control and being more aware.

The corporate world and the governments of the world are in bed with each other; we can turn the tables on them, no matter what country we live in. The same rules of supply and demand that cause discomfort in the general population can instead cause discomfort in government and the corporate world. When a large enough group of people affect the profit margins of big business and government in whatever country they are in, these entities pay attention. That is the power we have at this juncture in history. Our goal is to empower the people of the world with awareness and peace so the powers that be will see that we want less government, less consumerism, less resource use, less psychological marketing, and more peace.

Everyone needs to chip in to save the planet now—this is imperative. We hear so much about other countries growing and starting to use more resources as fast as Western nations do. We can influence new and emerging nations by living by example. We can stop relying on disposable products, and products made of plastic that will pollute our environment and never break down. We can create a market of earth-friendly products instead. The planet is caught up in a whirlwind of production of a disposable world. Production and consumerism is going so fast that the corporate world looks to produce products that are out of date three to six months after they hit the market. All of us have to start seeing the insanity of this. We need to be aware of how percentages, supply and demand, and profit-based marketing work and how we can affect what is happening in the world.

The corporate world reacts to trends and demands. They create them to fit their profit- driven models. They lobby and influence governments to get their way. They bully the world. How many times have we heard of companies and associations and corporations of all sorts telling the world they can't be allowed to fail and not make money? They argue that with fewer sales, everyone, including the government, will be hurt. All they are really saying is, "You cannot stop giving us your money. Help us, we need our massive profits." And of course they get it and then they tell us they are broke and give themselves a raise way past the cost of living each year. It goes on and on. And while they are saying this, corporate CEOs are making $10-50 million a year and more. It is out of hand and needs to change.

One of the saddest and most horrendous outcomes of the current system is war—war over oil, land, beliefs, false pride, egos, money, drugs, the marketing of certain products, etc. War is now big business that costs billions every year. Do not ever forget that someone is making all of that money. We need to be more aware and think about how much of that money is spent by the dream weavers stirring up emotion and sentiment to keep the insanity and war going. Don't think for a minute that part of the multi-billion dollar budget for the war is not going to influence our behaviors and distract us from what is really happening. The spin doctors know their business and they know it well.

Change toward peace is critical if we are going to survive and heal the planet. All of the steps in this book are possible and will make a difference. The more you do these steps, the bigger the change will be. Remember that many small steps will equal long distances. We all have to start doing something; even little things can change percentage points. Like we said, we know it won't come easy to many but to those who find it unimaginable, we ask you to look at the alternative to continuing the present way. Just start with yourself and your family. Then join other families. Look past the fear and see what your neighborhood can accomplish; you can be part of a greater thing. Enough people doing something will start to change those percentage points and reverse the cycle. It will be noticed—there will be meetings called in corporate boardrooms and in governments all over the world.

Our economy and financial infrastructure is much more fragile than what we are told. Look how the Federal Reserve can make a difference all over the world and on Wall Street by changing the interest rate to the banks in the United States just a quarter point. It is all in front of us; we just have to slow down and open our eyes to see it, and then make the decision to change things. So the way to deal with the present system is really not to deal with the system; at least not deal with the system as you have been doing. If you don't deal with corporate America, they will notice and they will start to listen and pay attention. They will then react and adapt. The government will follow suit.

We are not saying people need to totally unplug from the grid, just that they should use a lot less of it and make up the difference themselves. That is the beginning of the journey to spiritual survival. By grid we mean the cycle we are in now in relationship to resource use. By grid we also mean thought patterns that are drilled into us that we allow to control our desires and how we live. The grid and its influence has helped us form dependencies that have resulted in our overuse of resources and not being aware. We need to refuse to participate in this. Do not let talk and empty promises placate you; that is the old way of doing things. It makes us complacent, and when we get complacent, things don't change.

What needs to be done is to take knowledge from the past, knowledge from Eastern and Western wisdom, and knowledge from science and technology and combine it all. We need to live more spiritually then work together to save the planet and make sure no one lacks the essentials of life, so we can all live in peace. If everyone on the planet were to picture in their minds that we can and do have the power to demand what we want—to demand products that will last our lifetime and our children's lifetimes for a reasonable cost that do not end up in dumps, street gutters, and landfills, then it will happen. Tell the companies making these products that we demand that they stop fouling the air and dirtying the water. Stop using the word "pollution" and call the poisons that are killing the planet by the name that they are. Stop promoting a disposable world and start promoting a sustainable world.

Tell governments and the corporate world to stop promoting war and start promoting peace. If every neighborhood used less resources and less of the grid, someone would listen. Governments and the corporate world would see that people are indeed part of the earth and not something to manipulate and just make profit off of.

Think what it would be like to have your requests listened to and taken seriously. You would never again be subject to messages like, "Listen closely as our options have changed; you will never talk to a human and we do not care." It would be a different world.

CHAPTER 8

Raising Your Consciousness in Preparation for 2012

This chapter will be shocking and it was meant to be that way to emphasize the importance of the changes that are happening now and into 2012 and beyond. The messengers have stated this must be so. They told us to expect a lot of chaos, but they also told us how people can survive it. Here is what they told us:

"The chaos has already started but 2012 will be the peak of turmoil. After that time a spiritual wave will come upon the earth from the heavens. Those who accept the love and light will continue on that path. Those who choose not to accept for their own personal reasons will what you call 'go crazy' and be out of their minds trying to deal with their internal chaos. They will not be able to accept and break down the barriers of hate, competition, and all the programming that we have spoken of. They will wander the earth looking for peace when they need to stop moving and exert the energy to break down their internal walls.

CHAPTER 8

The chaos that you will witness after the year you call 2012 will not only entail outwardly chaos, fire, storms, stealing, and madness, but internal chaos dealing with these emotions. It will be a personal fire of burning the old ways of thinking, trying to steal and borrow the emotions that other people display, and the emotional turmoil of all of the environmental influences that your leaders have created. What you, the people have to deal with is the consequences of your behaviors that have lead to and are a distraction from living in the light, from the heart, and from nature."

Everyone must now push harder towards the spiritual side of life to become one with nature, and one with Earth's energy. Do not be afraid of the unknown. We have told you to give up your belongings because they will be of no value when the coming energy shifts occur. When the changes happen, there will be no fuel to use motor vehicles; there will be no electricity to use electronic devices. People must start to think about how life will be living without modern conveniences.

The changes coming will not be like when a disaster hits and people are inconvenienced for three days without power. This will go beyond that. People will have to think about what it will be like not to have fresh water at their fingertips and what it will be like to wait in long lines to get fresh water. Many people will have no fresh water or will not understand how to get it. They may have to stand in long lines to use an indoor toilet, or use the outdoors as a toilet for an extended period of time. People have taken for granted having light whenever they want it. The shock of losing all these things for an extended period will be overwhelming for many. There will be anger and blame and hatred and judging of others. There will be chaos.

We all must prepare to be and have love to deal with those who will be angry. We must fill ourselves with light to help us cope with those who will have hatred, depression, and other psychological ailments that will definitely have an effect on how they survive on Earth. Many without the psychological and spiritual training we have described will be lost and not know what to do or say or be. In the beginning, those who will be peaceful and follow love and kindness will have a much tougher time than those who will be filled with anger when for example fighting for food. The ones with anger will take what they want; that is the old way. Those who are peaceful will know love is also a part of us. People can develop and obtain food with both emotions, but one will be taking the path of peace, not the path of turmoil. So even though times will be hard at first for those filled with love, they will know it is the right way.

What you must ask of your higher power and spiritual guides is to help you achieve a higher level of consciousness. This means being more aware of your environment, your emotions, and being more spiritual. What does being more spiritual mean? It means living in the light—living your life through and with love, being peaceful, and treating yourself and everyone else peacefully. It means living with nature.

Recall from the past how other cultures maintained their way of living. You ask how they could possibly live without television, radio, video games, cell phones, and cars. Think about how these previous cultures lived throughout history without all these things. Every day and night examine every task you complete by means of what you use. For example, most of society, not counting the indigenous ones that still live in the jungle, use cooking with electricity or gas that is piped in to them or delivered. Everyone must start thinking about how to live without modern conveniences like electronic or gas stoves.

People also need to begin thinking about alternative fuels and the issues surrounding them if electricity and gas aren't going to be available. If everyone addressed this issue now, there would be enough alternative fuel available to prevent riots and stealing when the changes happen. Could you use solar power, and how could you get it into your home? What will you do with the stove and other electronic appliances that you have? Recycle them of course, but everyone needs to start to thinking about how that might work.

Without electricity and traditional energy sources, people will need to think about where they will find food and how they can grow their own when the supermarkets are empty. Now is the time for everyone to think and learn and do, and to prepare so that the shock of 2012 will not be so shocking. The most difficult part of this of course will be separating yourselves from knowing that electricity and water will always be available in your house. How will thousands of people get their water and from where and how will that water be transferred to community pools?

Parts of society will not be prepared for such changes. Those who are locked up in prisons have been out of touch with nature, and all their anger, chaos, and emotion, will cause more chaos and darkness. People who depend on electronic devices for their health will be severely impacted.

In the previous chapters of this book, we talked about material things and removing them. In 2012 this will become even more important because as the scenarios that have been described in this chapter unfold, people can raise their awareness and consciousness by sharing what they have with others. The kind of clothes you wear will not matter. Everyone will need to trust their instincts. Faith and trust will be needed; they are really one in the same when it comes to spiritual living.

We asked the messengers how the individual and/or the group should react, knowing that these changes are coming. We asked them how we can grasp what to do to be ready and prepared spiritually, physically, and emotionally? The answer is to change your level of consciousness, and study ways of surviving before all this comes to pass, although people who have increased their spiritual awareness will receive a measure of physical protection and guidance. Everyone will have the choice of whether to deal with the chaos in a peaceful manner or not, and to be aware enough to see that living in fear and other negative emotions will not be effective in getting their physical or spiritual needs met.

As the changes occur, an increased level of spirituality will create more balance in nature, in everyone's intuitiveness, and in the ability to live harmoniously with nature. That is why living in small communities and communicating with others who are like minded will provide guidance and learning to living more peacefully and spiritually; it will have a domino effect across humanity. The chaos will come to an end, but before it does and the world and all its inhabitants are raised to a higher consciousness, there will be what appears to be madness.

When chaos occurs, it will result from natural disasters and war. War will come when our assigned leaders lash out in fear of change and try to continue to control their environment as they know it. There will be some in all governments who will try to keep a semblance of balance during the peak of chaos. It does not matter if chaos is caused by war or by natural disaster. It is still chaos. War and natural disasters are reflective of each other. With both, there comes famine and a breakdown of the power grids and supply chains, resulting in stealing and other behaviors that are associated with those types of events. But chaos is a symptom of being out of balance. The natural disasters that happen are the heavens' way of stating the earth and its people are out of balance. War is also a symptom of what happens when the inhabitants of the world are out of balance.

Once balance and love have been restored in a sense, then the natural disasters will also diminish. The coming years will also be a time when everyone on Earth and the earth itself will have a chance to move forward spiritually and become a more peaceful and better place to live.

You all must take the responsibility of your new awareness very seriously. By that we mean that everyone must take what knowledge and wisdom they can from what has been written in this book, and act upon what they feel is important. We ask that even if you do not agree with all that is said here, try to keep an open mind and act on the part you do agree with. Be responsible. Start teaching your children survival skills along with all their other studies, and talk to them and others around you about your intuition and spirituality. Teach the skills of living by your intuition and instincts to your children and friends, and if you need teaching first seek that out. Teach them to trust in what they see and experience, and live according to what nature's voice is saying to them.

The time of the programmed mind is coming to an end. Make yourself available for service to others with compassion and remember, "There are many boats on the river." We are all different in ways, but the same in spirit, and we are all heading into the same future. Whatever that future holds for you, start now to create the karma to make it a future filled with peace and love.

Being responsible with the new awareness will help you alleviate the negatives and the feelings of being lost when the coming changes are more upon us. It will help you let go and allow the coming love and light to flow through you. There will be light workers and teachers and healers and guides that will be here to help and are filled with love and light and caring. Look to everyone as a possible teacher and teach what you can to others.

The time of fear, anger, and negative-based thinking is coming to an end in human history. Everyone will have to work together to get through the coming changes. Look around you, see all the changes on the earth, and see the changes in its people. Feel the earth rumbling and talking to you and crying out for help; see the sky fill with wind and rain. Acknowledge the frantic pace the world is experiencing. As people are responsible to their families and jobs and children, they must now also be responsible to themselves and the awareness that they need to prepare. We must all stop the destruction of the planet and everyone on it. But that is not enough; there is a higher mission of bringing peace and love to all who live on the earth and to Mother Earth herself—our home.

Live in light, love, and peace.

CHANGE HAS BEGUN

2008 ———————————————— 2012

MEET THE AUTHORS

MICHELLE KRAUS has worked in the Human Services field for over twelve years. Michelle is currently working for the Department of Human Services for the State of Minnesota. She graduated from Bemidji State University in Minnesota with a bachelors degree in Social Work with a minor in Sociology. Michelle grew up in a middle class family in a rural town of 7100 people in Northern Minnesota. During her college years, Michelle discovered that she had abilities that were outside the norm. She related these abilities to spiritual sources and began studying spiritual paths and information. Through dreams and senses she was able to be aware of events that others could not. The events caused Michelle to feel "different" and so she was uncomfortable speaking with anyone about these events, predictions and feelings and so she independently studied more about paths of spirituality to help her feel more at peace. In rural areas in the 1990's, being " different" was not acceptable. What happened made Michelle aware that there was something more than just the life we experience with our five senses. Michelle moved to Minneapolis and started working with developmentally disabled individuals. While working as a Service Planner, she met Jay who had just been hired with the same company. She felt compelled to speak with Jay concerning metaphysical matters. She felt this message came from her deceased brother. A relationship was developed based on metaphysical and spiritual discussion and lessons. Jay always seemed compelled to provide Michelle with a pertinent "lesson of the day." Michelle was warned by Jay that once you start a spiritual path it can be challenging and rewarding at the same time. Michelle continues her education regarding her spiritual development.

JAY HILL was raised in Minneapolis. Jay attended school for commercial foods in his early twenties and later management schooling on his way to becoming an Executive Chef, Restaurant Owner, Cannery Supervisor and working in Research and Development in the commercial food business. Jay spent almost thirty years working in the commercial food business before changing directions and seeking work in the human services field. At that point in his life Jay was aware he needed a profession with a more acceptable karma. He currently works in the human services field in the Minneapolis area working with developmentally disabled adults. Concerning spirituality, his family was Catholic and religious so Jay was exposed to organized religion at an early age. Jay was never comfortable with the doctrine and dogma of organized religion but for his mother's sake he attended church regularly till he moved away from home. Jay moved away from home at fifteen and went into the working world. As this was the late 60's and 70's, Jay was exposed to much change in the world. Jay experienced life to its fullest including difficult times with drugs and alcohol and all that entails. In his teens, Jay through good and bad times and not being happy with organized religion or the path his life was taking, began his search for a spiritual path that was acceptable to him, from the alpha wave training and relaxation systems of the times, to starting meditation and looking into eastern belief systems. Jay looked to experience them all. Jay felt a compelling urge to seek a way to finding peace in his life. Jay understood that friends and family and others did not seem to have this desire like he did. How they tried to influence him did not deter him from seeking his path. Even in his teens and twenties, Jay understood it would take spiritual influences, thinking and actions to make his life better and help him escape the cycles of negativity in his personnel life and due to the times. Jay understood the need for balance. Geographical change was part of Jay's seeking and part of his life. Seeking the greener grass. He traveled and lived through out the United States. During these times always seeking, he was exposed to many spiritual paths and philosophies from Buddhism to Charismatic beliefs. Jay's exposure to such a wide range of people, geographical areas and spirituality he feels helped him to find himself. Jay presently practices a mix of eastern and western beliefs to help him achieve balance in his life. Through out his lifetime, through meditation, constant independent study and discussion Jay has discovered a place of peace, acceptance and gratitude. His awareness and understanding that to live simply and spiritually has helped him help others.

APPENDIX

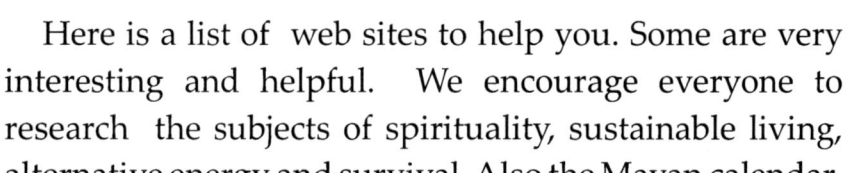

Here is a list of web sites to help you. Some are very interesting and helpful. We encourage everyone to research the subjects of spirituality, sustainable living, alternative energy and survival. Also the Mayan calendar, channeling and ancient civilizations. Buddhism, and meditation and awareness.

- Peace to all, MICHELLE AND JAY

www.drsmick.com   this is a very helpful and interesting site that deals with psychic work and spirituality. Sign up for the helpful monthly newsletter. Highly recommended.

www.greenpeace.org   This site is self explanatory. Greenpeace is a great organization.

www.innercirclepublishing.com This publisher only publishes spiritual and metaphysical books, like this one (smiles).

www.spiritual-endeavors.org Very good site with articles concerning world peace and has great info. Check out the Dali Llamas acceptance speech for the Nobel Peace Prize. All kinds of information from the 100th monkey effect to global peace meditations and channeling.

www.blogtalkradio.com/aware Part of InnerCircle Publishing, Jay Hill and Michelle Kraus have spiritual shows every Friday night on Aware talk Radio at 8:00 PM CST. Tune in and call in ... let us know what's on your mind.

www.writeandedit.com This site is Amy Farrar's the editor of this book. If you are interested in writing or have editing needs, just get a hold of Amy.

www.sustainable.org This site has a lot of good information on all aspects of sustainable living.

www.ssrsi.org That stands for "survival & self reliance" this site has a lot of information on canning and preserving food. plus safely handling food.

www.zombiehunters.org Another food preparation and storing site.

www.ala.org This site is the "association of college and research libraries" This site has lots about alternative energy, good site.

www.about.com Fun and informative site for everything from religions to food, good place to expand knowledge.

www.buddhnet.net Good site all about Buddhism.

www.meditatepeace.com Non-sectarian world meditation for everyone.

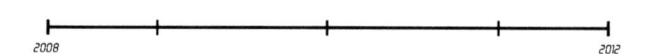

These are just a few websites to broaden your knowledge and awareness. Remember, if a site does not feel right for you you need not look into it. Go to site that resonates, one to which you are drawn. They contain information for you. There are some sites on the internet which contain misinformation on purpose. Be aware and you will feel that they are wrong. Remember to live with an open heart and open mind and that to be aware is to go protected into the night.

- Thanks, MICHELLE AND JAY

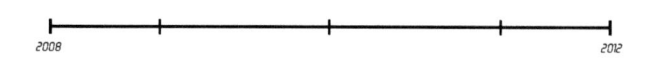

Aware Talk Radio

Join Us - LIVE - 7 Nights A Week!!!
Or Listen To Past Archvies @:
www.innercirclepublishing.com

http://www.blogtalkradio.com/aware

Call In Number: *(646) 716-8138*

    Aware Talk Radio incorporates all fields of science, from the normal to the paranormal, from the physical to the metaphysical. We seek to expand the awareness of humankind. Your Comments, Questions, and Guest Suggestions are welcome.

INNERCIRCLE PUBLISHING

Seeking Publication?

Are You Aware? Poet? Author of Metaphysical Content?

Contact InnerCircle Publishing

- Over 55 Metaphysical Titles in Print -
- World-Wide distribution via Ingram -
- Drop-Ship Abilities to any location on the planet -
- Active and Exponential Marketing for all Titles -
- World-Wide Radio Exposure -
- Automated Order Fulfillment for Customers and Booksellers -
- Authors Retain 100% of their Rights and Net Profits -
- Sales Compensation Paid Monthly -

Are You Aware?
www.innercirclepublishing.com